HAZARDING ALL

EDINBURGH CRITICAL STUDIES IN SHAKESPEARE AND PHILOSOPHY
Series Editor: Kevin Curran

Edinburgh Critical Studies in Shakespeare and Philosophy takes seriously the speculative and world-making properties of Shakespeare's art. Maintaining a broad view of 'philosophy' that accommodates first-order questions of metaphysics, ethics, politics and aesthetics, the series also expands our understanding of philosophy to include the unique kinds of theoretical work carried out by performance and poetry itself. These scholarly monographs will reinvigorate Shakespeare studies by opening new interdisciplinary conversations among scholars, artists and students.

Editorial Board Members
Ewan Fernie, Shakespeare Institute, University of Birmingham
James Kearney, University of California, Santa Barbara
Julia Reinhard Lupton, University of California, Irvine
Madhavi Menon, Ashoka University
Simon Palfrey, Oxford University
Tiffany Stern, Shakespeare Institute, University of Birmingham
Henry Turner, Rutgers University
Michael Witmore, The Folger Shakespeare Library
Paul Yachnin, McGill University

Published Titles
Rethinking Shakespeare's Political Philosophy: From Lear to Leviathan
Alex Schulman
Shakespeare in Hindsight: Counterfactual Thinking and Shakespearean Tragedy
Amir Khan
Second Death: Theatricalities of the Soul in Shakespeare's Drama
Donovan Sherman
Shakespeare's Fugitive Politics
Thomas P. Anderson
Is Shylock Jewish? Citing Scripture and the Moral Agency of Shakespeare's Jews
Sara Coodin
Chaste Value: Economic Crisis, Female Chastity and the Production of Social Difference on Shakespeare's Stage
Katherine Gillen
Shakespearean Melancholy: Philosophy, Form and the Transformation of Comedy
J. F. Bernard
Shakespeare's Moral Compass
Neema Parvini
Shakespeare and the Fall of the Roman Republic: Selfhood, Stoicism and Civil War
Patrick Gray
Revenge Tragedy and Classical Philosophy on the Early Modern Stage
Christopher Crosbie
Shakespeare and the Truth-Teller: Confronting the Cynic Ideal
David Hershinow
Derrida Reads Shakespeare
Chiara Alfano
Conceiving Desire: Metaphor, Cognition and Eros in Lyly and Shakespeare
Gillian Knoll
Immateriality and Early Modern English Literature: Shakespeare, Donne and Herbert
James A. Knapp
Hazarding All: Shakespeare and the Drama of Consciousness
Sanford Budick

Forthcoming Titles
Making Publics in Shakespeare's Playhouse
Paul Yachnin
The Play and the Thing: A Phenomenology of Shakespearean Theatre
Matthew Wagner
Shakespeare's Staging of the Self: The Reformation and Protestant Hermenuetics
Roberta Kwan

For further information please visit our website at: edinburghuniversitypress.com/series/ecsst

HAZARDING ALL

Shakespeare and the Drama of Consciousness

◆ ◆ ◆

SANFORD BUDICK

EDINBURGH
University Press

Edinburgh University Press is one of the leading university presses in the UK. We publish academic books and journals in our selected subject areas across the humanities and social sciences, combining cutting-edge scholarship with high editorial and production values to produce academic works of lasting importance. For more information visit our website: edinburghuniversitypress.com

© Sanford Budick, 2021, 2023

Edinburgh University Press Ltd
The Tun – Holyrood Road, 12(2f) Jackson's Entry, Edinburgh EH8 8PJ

First published in hardback by Edinburgh University Press 2021

Typeset in 12/15 Adobe Sabon by
IDSUK (DataConnection) Ltd

A CIP record for this book is available from the British Library

ISBN 978 1 4744 9315 4 (hardback)
ISBN 978 1 4744 9316 1 (paperback)
ISBN 978 1 4744 9317 8 (webready PDF)
ISBN 978 1 4744 9318 5 (epub)

The right of Sanford Budick to be identified as the author of this work has been asserted in accordance with the Copyright, Designs and Patents Act 1988, and the Copyright and Related Rights Regulations 2003 (SI No. 2498).

CONTENTS

Acknowledgements		vii
Series Editor's Preface		xi
1.	Terms of Discussion	1
2.	'Conversion' of the 'Nothing' by the Instrumentality of *The Merchant of Venice*	33
3.	Towards an Escape from Theatricalisation: *Hamlet* and *As You Like It*	55
4.	The Second *Epoché* of *Othello* and *The Merchant of Venice*	93
5.	Intentionality toward Being: Blessing in *King Lear* and *The Winter's Tale*	111
Retrospect		155
Bibliography		159
Index		167

For Emily

and for Stephen and Annette Hochstein

ACKNOWLEDGEMENTS

During the course of work on this book, stimulating comments and questions of auditors to lecture presentations have put me in debt in ways too detailed and too numerous to list here. Yet for especially generous encouragement and aid at various stages, I need to offer explicit thanks to Kevin Curran, James Dale, Stephen Fallon, Stephen Hochstein, Michael Kaufman, Julia Reinhard Lupton, Henry Weinfield and Jon Whitman.

Earlier versions of some of the chapters appeared in the following volumes: *Religious Diversity and Early Modern English Texts: Catholic, Judaic, Feminist, and Secular Dimensions*, ed. Arthur F. Marotti and Chanita Goodblatt (Detroit: Wayne State University Press, 2013), pp. 330–51; *Shakespeare and Judgment*, ed. Kevin Curran (Edinburgh: Edinburgh University Press, 2017), pp. 195–214; *Shakespeare's Hamlet: Philosophical Perspectives*, ed. Tzachi Zamir (New York: Oxford University Press, 2018), pp. 130–53; and *Entertaining the Idea: Shakespeare, Philosophy, and Performance*, ed. Lowell Gallagher, James Kearney and Julia Reinhard Lupton (Toronto: University of Toronto Press, 2021), pp. 135–64.

SERIES EDITOR'S PREFACE

Picture Macbeth alone on stage, staring intently into empty space. 'Is this a dagger which I see before me?' he asks, grasping decisively at the air. On one hand, this is a quintessentially theatrical question. At once an object and a vector, the dagger describes the possibility of knowledge ('Is this a dagger') in specifically visual and spatial terms ('which I see before me'). At the same time, Macbeth is posing a quintessentially philosophical question, one that assumes knowledge to be both conditional and experiential, and that probes the relationship between certainty and perception as well as intention and action. It is from this shared ground of art and inquiry, of theatre and theory, that this series advances its basic premise: Shakespeare is philosophical.

It seems like a simple enough claim. But what does it mean exactly, beyond the parameters of this specific moment in *Macbeth*? Does it mean that Shakespeare had something we could think of as his own philosophy? Does it mean that he was influenced by particular philosophical schools, texts and thinkers? Does it mean, conversely, that modern philosophers have been influenced by *him*, that Shakespeare's plays and poems have been, and continue to be, resources for philosophical thought and speculation?

The answer is yes all around. These are all useful ways of conceiving a philosophical Shakespeare and all point to lines of inquiry that this series welcomes. But Shakespeare is philosophical in a much more fundamental way as well. Shakespeare is philosophical because the plays and poems actively create new worlds of knowledge and new scenes of ethical encounter. They ask big questions, make bold arguments and develop new vocabularies in order to think what might otherwise be unthinkable. Through both their scenarios and their imagery, the plays and poems engage the qualities of consciousness, the consequences of human action, the phenomenology of motive and attention, the conditions of personhood and the relationship among different orders of reality and experience. This is writing and dramaturgy, moreover, that consistently experiments with a broad range of conceptual crossings, between love and subjectivity, nature and politics, and temporality and form.

Edinburgh Critical Studies in Shakespeare and Philosophy takes seriously these speculative and world-making dimensions of Shakespeare's work. The series proceeds from a core conviction that art's capacity to think – to formulate, not just reflect, ideas – is what makes it urgent and valuable. Art matters because unlike other human activities it establishes its own frame of reference, reminding us that all acts of creation – biological, political, intellectual and amorous – are grounded in imagination. This is a far cry from business-as-usual in Shakespeare studies. Because historicism remains the methodological gold standard of the field, far more energy has been invested in exploring what Shakespeare once meant than in thinking rigorously about what Shakespeare continues to make possible. In response, Edinburgh Critical Studies in Shakespeare and Philosophy pushes back against the critical orthodoxies of historicism and cultural studies to clear a space for scholarship that confronts aspects of literature that can neither be reduced to nor adequately explained by particular historical contexts.

Shakespeare's creations are not just inheritances of a past culture, frozen artefacts whose original settings must be expertly reconstructed in order to be understood. The plays and poems are also living art, vital thought-worlds that struggle, across time, with foundational questions of metaphysics, ethics, politics and aesthetics. With this orientation in mind, Edinburgh Critical Studies in Shakespeare and Philosophy offers a series of scholarly monographs that will reinvigorate Shakespeare studies by opening new interdisciplinary conversations among scholars, artists and students.

Kevin Curran

'let me still remain / The true blank of thine eye'

Kent to Lear

CHAPTER 1

TERMS OF DISCUSSION

The Reach of Shakespeare's 'Negative Capability'

Commentators have long struggled to salvage the insights within Keats's striking but vague remarks about the 'quality' that Shakespeare 'possessed so enormously' – '*Negative Capability*'. Keats said that he meant by this that Shakespeare was 'capable of being in uncertainties, Mysteries, doubts, without any irritable reaching after fact & reason'.[1] Keats gave concrete expression to his own imagination of this kind, saying, 'if a Sparrow come before my Window I take part in its existence [*sic*] and pick about the Gravel.'[2] Walter Jackson Bate pondered these remarks over a lifetime and concluded that 'taken by themselves they could lead almost anywhere'. He added, however, that Keats here registered his intuition of the acts that Shakespeare's (the great poet's) 'Negative Capability' tangibly performs: 'negating one's own ego' and producing 'the harmony of the human imagination and its object'.[3] Keats did not begin to explain how either of these acts might be carried out in poetic practice. Yet I believe that together these acts do indeed create one principal kind of Shakespearean consciousness and that their effectuation in his plays is accessible to detailed textual exposition as well as to systematic philosophical elucidation.

I propose that that which Keats wished to see as the easy flow from a 'quality' of the poet's personality to representation that expresses that personality is by Shakespeare earned through varieties of arduous *negative* representation. Shakespeare unfolds his achievement of the negative in a systematic language of the 'nothing'. In Shakespeare's and the spectator's partnered hands, this language enables both the negation of a solipsistic ego – in the self as well as other – and the production of an imaginative harmony between the self and its object or other. In the plays that I will discuss these achievements are sometimes incipiently at work in the minds of protagonists, but more often and more fully they are to be found in the shared consciousness that the plays create between Shakespeare and the spectator. To attain this intersubjective consciousness, Shakespeare and this special kind of spectator both pass into the condition of *onlookers*. This they achieve through the instrumentality of the 'nothing' that, reaching beyond the plays themselves, suspends theatricalisation – theatrical representation itself – while creating another kind of representation. The force of Hamlet's outcry against the glass cage of theatricalisation, that it is 'All for nothing' ('What's Hecuba to him, or he to her, / That he should weep for her?' (2.2.492–5)), will point Shakespeare and the spectator beyond Hamlet and *Hamlet* toward an exit from theatre itself.[4] Stanley Cavell notes Hamlet's 'ceaseless perception of theatre . . . as an inescapable or metaphysical mark of the human condition, together with his endless sense of debarment from accepting the human condition as his'. Cavell couples this remark with another concerning Hamlet's desire to escape the metaphysical mark of this theatricality:

> [Shakespeare's] particular dramaturgical structure, or discovery, I shall call deferred representation; Shakespeare's way of representing in the closing image of a play something denied our sight from the beginning . . . a scene, let me say, metaphysically invisible before this time and place.[5]

I believe this observation is of the utmost importance. 'Deferred representation' is at the deepest heart of Shakespeare's mature theatricality. I propose, however, that this deferred representation culminates in his overleaping of theatricality, by means of theatricality, to access a scene that until now has been metaphysically invisible. Strange as it may at first seem, I believe, and will demonstrate, that Shakespeare and the spectator achieve the exit to such a scene only from the combined work of deferred representation in two partnered plays. Only the interactions of two such plays together, reciprocally, can neutralise the fictiveness of theatricality and open upon a scene, an object, of conceptual reflection. I will show how Shakespeare first achieved this double deferral of representation, and this exit to a standpoint of reflection on representation, in the mirror relation between *Hamlet* and *As You Like It*.

At the risk of getting ahead of what I will show and explain hereafter, I will already propose what I consider to be the grounds of Shakespeare's achievements by his *Capability* of the *Negative*. At the base of those achievements is Shakespeare's recognition that theatrical representation (indeed, any representation) – no matter how multiplex and no matter how populated by innumerable interrelations of individual protagonists – ultimately expresses a fantasy projection of a controlling ego and its lone consciousness or subjectivity. For Shakespeare the aim of ultimately exiting theatricalisation is totally different from an exclusionary anti-theatrical prejudice. On the contrary, Shakespeare, pre-eminently, recognises the necessity of engaging and working through the inevitable theatricalisations of human imagination that are part of all human experience. In the pairings of the plays I will discuss, this exit from theatre is accomplished by the suspensive effect of mirrorings between the plays in the given pair. Along with the exit from theatre, the same mirrorings create the playwright's and the spectator's place to stand outside theatre and outside one's individual subjectivity in an intersubjective, fully equal relationship.

4] Hazarding All

The Language of the 'Nothing'

Shakespeare deploys two inversive kinds of 'nothing' that are at first sight undifferentiable. The inward, unworldly 'nothing' is magisterially exemplified by Cordelia's 'Nothing, my lord' (1.182) spoken from a yet to be understood fullness of personality and love. The purely worldly, ultimately empty, 'nothing' which would wipe out the unworldly 'nothing' and its demands is exemplified by Edmond's seemingly identical 'Nothing, my lord' (1.2.31). Our own schooling in the syntagmas of the 'nothing' gradually makes it possible to see that Edmond's 'nothing' is indeed 'nothing like [i.e. the nothing that is like] the image and horror of it' (1.3.147–8) in that it is always attended by a repressed *horror vacui* of the worldly 'nothing' itself. Cordelia's unworldly 'nothing', which Lear is initially incapable of recognising much less understanding, does more than set the tragedy of *King Lear* on its irreversible course. After the defeat of the worldly 'nothing' in the anagnorisis of the tragedy, the same unworldly 'nothing' propels our experience of the play towards a fuller realisation of human consciousness.

In these plays the conversion of the worldly, empty 'nothing' is effected in a transmuted linguistic medium. In this language the unworldly 'nothing' becomes the sign of a substantive condition. Such are Kent's 'Nothing almost sees miracles / But misery' (2.2.148–9) and Edgar's 'Edgar I nothing am' (2.3.21) or 'In nothing am I changed' (4.5.8). These tormented phrases point towards a secular trans-substantiation of the 'nothing' through humiliation and suffering. Lear has not himself fully attained that conversion even when he echoes Cordelia's 'nothing' in the third act: 'No, I will be the pattern of all patience. / I will say nothing' (3.2.35–6). I suggest that the powers of this 'nothing' are the same as those Hamlet gradually discloses in the 'All for nothing' of theatricalisation (2.2.494) and those that Orlando and Rosalind will discover, respectively and mutually, in the 'nothing' (1.2.151) and 'lack' (4.1.142) that are at the heart of their capacity for creating meaning and love. In *The Winter's Tale* (in my view, the partner play to *King Lear*) Leontes's blind, Lear-like insistence on the solidity of the worldly 'nothing' (1.2.289–93), which triggers his personal tragedy, provides the defining contrast for the play's unworldly 'nothing'. Florizel points – beyond his own explicit awareness – to the secret of Perdita's abiding in an unworldly 'nothing' when he says to her, 'I wish you / A wave o' the sea, that you might even *do / Nothing* but that: move still, still so' (4.4.140–3; emphases added), just as Polixenes says far more than he knows when he observes of Perdita, '*Nothing she does* or seems / But smacks of something greater than herself' (4.4.157–8; emphases added). Perdita, who *does* this 'nothing', will herself signal one near completion of the journey toward Shakespearean consciousness when she echoes Cordelia's 'nothing': 'I cannot speak / So well, *nothing* so well' (4.4.360–1; emphases added).

Suspension and the 'Now'

My view of Shakespeare's language of the 'nothing' in *Hamlet* is complementary to, but revises, Stephen Greenblatt's important observation that in '*Hamlet* Shakespeare made a discovery by means of which he relaunched his entire career. The crucial breakthrough . . . had to do . . . with an intense representation of inwardness by a new technique of radical excision', by which Greenblatt means 'occluding the rationale, motivation, or ethical principle that accounted for the action to be unfolded'. Greenblatt adds that side by side with this 'excision' and 'suspension' Shakespeare creates a 'strange interim'.[6] I propose that the chief technique of radical excision in *Hamlet* is Hamlet's use of chiasmus.[7] The key to seeing the extent and significance of chiasmus in Hamlet's language is to recognise that he finds himself, throughout, in an agonising condition of cross purposes that takes chiastic form and which he repeatedly locates in the dilemmas of theatricalisation. Hamlet shows how a chiasmus of theatricalisation lies in wait within the human imagination itself and how, by facing its challenges 'swift as meditation' (1.5.29– 30), something far more important than revenge can be achieved. Hamlet harnesses the power of meditative chiasmus to produce consciousness of a negative space (that which philosophers since Hegel call a 'negativity') within representation, where the atemporal presentation of his self, or inward being, can be disclosed. By the imagination's inherent theatricalisation I mean the back-and-forth movements between role-playing consciousness and a would-be non-role-playing consciousness that is never free from role-playing. Shakespeare's use of chiasmus in these plays everywhere follows Hamlet's meditative employment – his productive thinking – of chiasmus, AB:BA. This is his holding of a theatricalising 'mirror up to nature' – reversing, in profound effect, the perception of left to right, right to left.[8]

The impact of chiasmus stems from the fact that its elements necessarily form an effectively infinite progression because, as Lisa Freinkel puts it, 'Repetition becomes inversion and inversion takes us back to where we started', so that chiasmus initiates 'an exchange that seems to have no beginning and no end'.[9] Arguably (as has indeed often been claimed in a variety of ways) such chiastic exchange is part of all conscious perception of sameness and difference, since every perception of sameness opens to differentiation and then every perception of difference opens to finding the common denominator of sameness, in endless progressions that circle around the object that interminably resists closure or totalisation.[10] Hamlet's representations, to himself, of his – and his world's – chiastic condition constitute repeated attempts to grasp the totality of infinite progressions and they repeatedly produce momentary inhibitions or suspensions of consciousness of the immediate external world. In other words, in Hamlet's hands chiasmus becomes a compact, portable engine of infinite progression and of experiencing the impossibility of grasping the totality of such a progression.

Judging by the intensity of Hamlet's recurrences to chiasmus we may well conclude that he knows or at least senses the blessings it can confer. He knows or senses that the initial failure it entails can ultimately leave him with the residual consciousness, most especially, of a self in an inward *now*. Chiasmus is the 'foolish figure' that Polonius pedantically identifies in Hamlet's apparently mad condition but entirely fails to see is at the heart of Hamlet's construction of consciousness. Thus in *Hamlet* – and *in The Merchant of Venice, Othello, As You Like It, King Lear* and *The Winter's Tale* – chiasmus reflects an inner drama of the search for meaning. It explores the dizzying way the elements that figure identity and difference turn not against but within language to produce a space of negativity where freedom of self or subjectivity can be disclosed. Hamlet knows or senses that, paradoxically, the use of this instrument of momentary suspension can ultimately furnish the grounds for his experience, as well as action, in the world. Indeed, one of the abiding, creative paradoxes of Hamlet's thinking (and his grasp of his – of humanity's – condition) is again and again centred in the back and forth movements of his theatrical chiasmata: these repeatedly manifest a resolute purposiveness within apparent vacillation. This paradox reaches a climax in his 'If it be . . .' clauses concerning the *now*, in Act 5. I will yet return to these clauses, but I note already that they, too, are tightly driven by the effects of chiasmus in producing an atemporal space (a strange interim) of the now. This 'now' emerges within the thematisations of the chronological now: 'If it [A] be now, 'tis [B] not to come. If it be [B] not to come, it will [A] be now' (5.2.198–9).[11]

Hamlet's most significant use of the chiasmus of theatricalisation – serving virtually as a template for all his other employments of this figure – is his self-accusatory question concerning the player's capacity to feel and to express emotion. After asking about that emotion, 'all for nothing – For Hecuba?' he asks further:

> What's [A] Hecuba to [B] him, or [B] he to [A] her,
> That he should weep for her? (2.2.492–4)

Horatio unwittingly provides an important clue to Hamlet's enigmatic ways of creating meaning when he describes the language of Hamlet's retreat into theatrical disguise as 'whirling words' (1.2.132). These chiastic whirling words consist of a layering of *play-acting* upon *would-be non-play-acting*, then again upon *would-be non-play-acting* upon *play-acting*, ad infinitum. The many chiasmata that Hamlet generates create a continual whirling spiral of this kind. The configuration of the Hecuba chiasmus thus encompasses the mind's, the imagination's, interminable interchange between kinds of role-playing in the quest for authenticity of self:

> *play-acting* (experiencing Hecuba in the fiction) to *would-be non-play-acting* ('him', the live actor, in real existence) // *would-be non-play-acting* ('he' the live actor) to *play-acting* ('her' in the fiction).

In this chiasmus of kinds of play-acting – of theatricalisation – that would locate an authentic self, a chiastic play of another kind is deeply implicit. This is the chiastic play of *other and self // self and other*: other ('Hecuba') / self ('him', the actor) // self ('he', the actor) / other ('Hecuba'). And the product of both of these layered chiasmata, as of *all* Hamlet's chiasmata, is the negative space, the 'nothing'. These nothings not only mark but themselves constitute moments of liminality of a mind in sharp transition. In the discussions of the plays that here concern us, we will see that the chiasmata of protagonists function as points of apostrophic concentration – to some extent of the protagonists themselves but, finally, and more fully of the playwright and spectator – that momentarily interrupt chronological time.[12] These moments achieve an intentionality and transmutation of meanings. (I will later return to the topic of intentionality.) Once we have become aware of the directionality of Hamlet's whirling words we sense the coming-into-being of various chiastic moments that are sometimes left hanging in mid-air. We may not spontaneously agree that a particular chiastic moment has been fully broached or opened. Yet, in *Hamlet* as in the other plays I will be discussing, the force of chiasmus is rendered pervasively potential by the deeply embedded chiasmus of theatricalisation. In other words, that chiasmus that serves as a scrim between the spectator (or reader) and the patterned language of theatricalisation.

I will soon explain how Shakespeare's momentary suspensions of human consciousness (principally achieved by chiastic language) are illuminated by Edmund Husserl's account of a meditative 'bracketing' that produces the space of the negative which he famously called the '*epoché*'. Before turning to Husserl I wish to emphasise that my aim in applying to his ideas is not to find the ways in which Shakespeare's practice matches Husserl's theories. Husserl, in my view, amalgamated a coherent schema from meditative concepts and practices that were already available, in their elements, to Shakespeare. Yet, even while Husserl perceived what those elements and their successive ordering had to be, he himself did not, or could not, bring them to realisation as acts of consciousness. To a great extent, therefore, the achieved increments of Shakespearean consciousness that are my subject are precisely goals that Husserl failed to achieve even though he saw with great clarity what they had to be. This failure is foreshadowed even in Husserl's meditative moment of setting out the requirement of a 'bracketing' for which he does not, or cannot, provide concrete means. As I will explain below, I believe this omission reflects Husserl's inability to locate an agent of the bracketing who would not already be in a relation of inequality with a hoped for intersubjective partner.

The concrete efficacy of Shakespeare's chiasmus, ultimately even of any chiasmus that is shared intersubjectively, is precisely in producing just such a bracketing and its space of the negative. In fact, a philosophical account of this efficacy is not far to seek. As Husserl surely realised but did not acknowledge, Kant supplied just such a means for producing something closely equivalent to the *epoché* – and to Shakespeare's 'nothing' of chiasmus. Kant did so in his writings on the sublime (specifically in what he calls the 'mathematically sublime') where his serviceability with regard to Shakespeare is not surprising since he elsewhere identified Shakespeare (with Milton) as one of the two great modern geniuses of the sublime.[13] For Kant an experience of the sublime and of the space of the negative are intertwined.

In the 'Analytic of the Sublime' of the third *Critique*, Kant described an experience of 'a momentary inhibition [or *check* or *restraint*]' ('*einer augenblicklichen Hemmung*') of consciousness that runs parallel to his account of a transcendental deduction in the first *Critique*. It, too, amounts to a transcendental deduction in that, after the 'inhibition' or 'check', the mind recovers an 'immediately following and all the more powerful' consciousness of its independent powers, particularly of its freedom and moral feeling (5: 245, 313, 318).[14] Judgement on the sublime, Kant says, is '*a priori*' – in his terms, transcendental – and 'immediately contains the deduction' (5: 280). He explains that the suspension of consciousness of the external world in the sublime is occasioned by a particular kind of aesthetic encounter, namely of trying, and failing, to grasp the totality of an effectively endless progression of items in a given field of consciousness (5: 250). Encounters of this kind, he argues, are most familiar in experiences of natural phenomena but he makes clear that they are also to be found in experiences of works of art.[15] In other words, in such aesthetic encounters the mind's chosen act of momentarily bracketing consciousness of the world is enabled by the momentary 'inhibition' – '*Hemmung*' – of consciousness. Kant's great insight here is that this *Hemmung* results from the clash of two of the mind's principal faculties, imagination and reason, in attempting, and failing, to grasp the totality of an infinite progression. Kant does not try to specify the degree of blockage in this inhibition of consciousness. Yet it is clear that in the momentary condition that is produced in this way the mind experiences a suspension of the world's spatio-temporality, in effect a negativity in which the residual self reposes in its own special temporality – having *removed*, Kant says, 'the time condition' (5: 258–9). In Freinkel's analysis of an exemplary exhibit of chiasmus she notes that it 'precludes a *present* ... The *now* itself ... is lost', leaving, she says, an 'odd temporality'.[16] I believe that this observation is both correct and significant, and that it is generalisable to all usages of the figure of chiasmus. Yet what Freinkel has seen here pertains to the precluded *present* and lost *now* of chronological temporality. From the perspectives of Kant's analysis of the inhibition of consciousness in confronting the infinite progression, we can see that it is exactly the suspension of chronological temporality that opens the uniquely odd temporality. This is a new temporality that is atemporal with respect to chronological time. This is the *presence* and *now* of the *epoché*. Paul de Man claimed that chiasmus 'can only come into being as the result of a void, of a lack that allows for the rotating motion of the polarities'.[17] The dynamic of the Kantian sublime strongly suggests that the precise opposite is the case. It is the endless progression in 'the rotating motion of the polarities' that itself produces the 'void' or 'lack', the negative space of a negativity and atemporality in the mind that performs the chiasmus.

Shakespeare and the Intentionality of Chiasmus

I will soon locate the pivotal importance of intentionality in Husserl's thinking. At this point it is important to note, quite independently of Husserl's ideas, the importance of directed or intentional reflection in Shakespeare's deployments of chiasmus. The intentionality of the speaker of chiasmus determines whether the consciousness of the 'nothing' that is produced by the chiasmus is directed toward *being, specifically the being of an other*, or – the starkly alternative choice – toward *non-being*, in worldly terms, *death*.[18] In Shakespeare's worlds of the 'nothing' one of its potentialities is that it can be directed as a force of mortification toward a helpless other. The extreme case of this kind of deadly intentionality is exemplified by Iago's directing of his chiasmus and its 'nothing' toward Othello's non-being and death, as in the third line of the following exchange between Iago and Othello (upon seeing Cassio depart from an interview, covertly arranged by Iago, with Desdemona):

> IAGO: Ha, I like not *that*.
> OTHELLO: What dost thou say?
> IAGO: *Nothing, my lord; or if – I know not what.*
> (3.3.35–7; emphases added)

Iago's chiastic thought twists the simple deictic 'that' into the unknowable 'what' of the 'nothing' – the 'nothing' or negative space of Othello's imagining of the space of Desdemona's sexuality. From his chiasmus, Iago generates the entangling imaginative experience of the space of that 'nothing' and directs it toward Othello as an entangling force (a curse) of non-being – transformed from the very space where human being originates:

> [A] that . . . Nothing, my lord;
> [B] or if –
> [B] I know not
> [A] what.

Shakespeare also shows a diametrically opposed possibility for the intentionality of chiasmus. Thus an intentionality of chiasmus and consciousness *toward being*, specifically toward the being of an other, is exemplified by Gloucester's words blessing Edgar just before Gloucester leaps from what he thinks is the cliff at Dover. Gloucester does not know – but the spectator does – that Edgar is the 'fellow' whom he is also blessing 'fare thee well'. And all this takes place in a moment of the *now* that the chiasmus not only names but produces:

> If [A] *Edgar* live, bless [B] him.
> Now, [B] fellow, fare [A] *thee* well. (4.5.41–2; emphasis added)

So, too, and even more so, Cordelia's intentionality of chiasmus, and its 'nothing', toward being, is produced within a reciprocity that, for Shakespeare, constitutes human 'benediction' – human *bene-dicere* toward each other:

> [A] O look upon me, [B] sir,
> And [B] hold your hand in benediction [A] o'er me. (4.6.54–5)[19]

In the plays before us the negative space of the atemporal *now* is the locus of the onlooker. Such an onlooker directs the 'nothing' toward being and herself or himself stands in the now of being. Shakespeare repeatedly produces such onlookers who stand outside, or beside – in that sense, at least, *transcendental* to – their worlds. The movement towards such onlooking is made explicit not only in Hamlet the director/spectator, but, in *As You Like It*, in Rosalind the spectator to the play-acting that she oversees and then, as epilogist, views over her shoulder – as well as in Hymen, an onlooker from a yet greater height. This dynamics of spectatorship is in *King Lear* extended (by Edgar and Cordelia as well as by Lear's desire to serve with Cordelia as 'God's spies', 5.3.17), in tandem with *The Winter's Tale*.[20] Perdita even refers to herself as a 'looker-on' (5.3.85). Perdita the onlooker brings into focus and begins to explain, in Husserlian terms, A. D. Nuttall's sense that in this play 'theatricality proves to be a mere paper screen, to be torn asunder by natural fact ... Theatricality is made to serve as a foil for something other than it.'[21] 'Natural fact' and a 'something other' on this order are strenuously earned by Shakespeare. To tear theatricality asunder is, in Husserl's terms, to 'blast open captivation-in-an-acceptedness' and thereby to enable acts of reflection directed to those natural facts, so that 'we are now living completely in such acts of the second degree'.[22]

For Shakespeare's account of human consciousness, a concept of the onlooker is indeed of vital importance. We will see that the attainment to an intersubjectivity by Shakespeare the onlooker and the spectator-onlooker spells the fruition of all aspects of Shakespeare's negative capability. In *King Lear*, Kent's words spoken to Lear, 'let me still remain / The true blank of thine eye' (which I have taken as the epigraph for this book) are also, and more efficaciously, Shakespeare's words directed to the spectator (1.1.152–3). The word 'still', which may seem redundant before 'remain', points to a now or presence within a motionless place of the negative. Far more than a metaphor drawn from archery, this is a 'blank' or 'nothing' within consciousness, the enabling of a condition that Kent and Lear might have experienced together, although they never do. This experience of subtraction to a zero, which both Shakespeare and the spectator undergo, is strongly hinted in the words 'remain' and 'blank'. In addition, the potential for an intersubjective consciousness is suggested by the possibility of a joint seeing of the 'true blank'. A joint seeing of this kind might have taken place reciprocally, that is through each other's eyes.[23] Such reciprocity of onlooking is the condition that Shakespeare and the spectator finally share.

*

Virtually all of the Shakespearean insights that I have begun to set out above have close parallels in the meditative line of phenomenology, beginning with Husserl, that leads (at least in Sartre's view) into existentialism. These Shakespearean-Husserlian correspondences obtain, that is, with regard to all the incremental means of extending consciousness of being itself. These are: an act of excision or suspension that opens a space of the negative or 'nothing' and an atemporal 'now'; disclosure of an inward self; transformation (conversion) into the condition of the onlooker; effecting an intentionality of chiasmus toward non-being or toward being; and, finally, the creation of an intersubjectivity. Even Shakespeare's deployment of chiasmus, which for him is the motor that drives and makes possible all of the above and which has no equivalent in Husserl, finds explicit parallels in a separate track of thinking the 'chiasm' within the unfolding meditative lines of phenomenology and existentialism.[24] In the plays discussed here, Shakespeare's increments of consciousness result from combining the equivalent of these two tracks: that is, the track of the *suspension* that opens the *'nothing'* (the philosophers' 'bracketing' that opens the *'epoché'* or *Nichts* or *Néant*) with the track of thinking the chiasm. Noting the parallels and divergences between Shakespeare and the philosophers in this launching ground of consciousness is by no means of merely archival interest. For one thing, these detached philosophical perspectives can provide a descriptive language that is released from the spellbinding impact of the physical or imagined theatrical stage. Carefully brought to bear, a philosophical language can thus open the way to understanding Shakespeare's almost invisible ways of advancing the horizon of human consciousness. Far more valuable, however, is that delving the parallels – and shortfalls – in the philosophers' accounts will locate the instances where Shakespeare already saw more deeply, already exceeded them, in the same tracks of intuition that they were to pursue – and where he already put those deeper intuitions into a practice that provided lived experience.

Negativity and Husserl's 'Reduction' and 'Epoché'

Under a variety of names, awareness of a space of the negative within thought and representation has been continuously in vivid evidence since antiquity; so, too, has been recognition of the potentiality of such 'negativity' for disclosing the self.[25] Striking examples of this are at work in the *khôra* of Plato's *Timaeus* and of Sophocles's *Oedipus at Colonus* (to which I will later turn) or, in the East, in the Patanjali Yoga Sutras where suspension of consciousness of the world opens the '*atha*' or 'Now' of the self. Husserl, in fact, was aware of the parallelism between Yoga and the phenomenological bracketing and '*epoché*' that disclose the transcendental self in what he also called its 'Now'.[26] Besides Kant's '*Hemmung*' ('check') and suspension and Husserl's *epoché*, the impact of negativity, of an achieved 'nothing', were variously registered in Descartes's application to a 'hyperbolical doubt' that leaves standing an 'I think' as well as in such later derivatives of Husserl's thought as Martin Heidegger's *Nichts* and Jean-Paul Sartre's *Néant*.[27] We need not force these varieties of awareness of negativity into one identical meaning in order to recognise the powerful significance of the idea of negativity before and after Shakespeare. In Keats's idea of a 'Negative Capability' he glimpses this negativity but, as we have noted, he does not stay to consider the systematic ways Shakespeare accesses it to build human consciousness.

Husserl early identified a 'dormant actuality [*Inaktualität*]' that is 'ever prepared to pass into the wakeful mode' of a 'focal actuality [*Aktualität*]'.[28] And he elaborated the ways in which awareness of this actuality is paradoxically dependent on the struggle to think with negativity, with a *Nichts* or '*nothing*'. For him this meant the employment of bracketing and *epoché*-centred structures of thought that build consciousness in acknowledgment of the unrepresentable dimension of language and of reality. Here, gathered from Husserl's explanations and those that he approved in the work of his close associate, Eugen Fink, are the terms and concepts of Husserl's method of a negativity-centred reflection. In these glosses we should not be thrown by the term 'phenomenological' which, given the functional directness of these explanations of that which is 'phenomenological', is here virtually redundant:

1. *The natural attitude and the phenomenological attitude*

   In the natural attitude we simply effect all the acts by virtue of which the world is there for us. We live naively in perceiving and experiencing, in these acts of positing in which unities <and realities of every kind> appear and not only appear but also are given with the characteristic of things [that seem] 'on hand', 'actual' ... In the phenomenological attitude ... we *prevent the effecting* of all such cogitative positings, i.e. we 'parenthesise' [bracket] the positings effected; ... Instead of living *in* them, instead of effecting *them*, we effect acts of *reflection* directed to them ... We are now living completely in such acts of the second degree.[29]

> Epoché [bracketing] and the reduction proper [carried out in intentional, directed acts of reflection] are the two internal *basic moments* of the phenomenological reduction, mutually required and mutually conditioned . . . in which we *blast open captivation-in-an-acceptedness* and first recognise the acceptedness as an acceptedness in the first place.[30]

2. *Un-humanising and the onlooker*[31]

In the universal **epoché**, in the disconnection of all belief-positings, the phenomenological onlooker produces himself. The transcendental tendency that awakens in man and drives him to inhibit all acceptednesses nullifies man himself; man *un-humanises* [*entmenscht*] himself in performing the **epoché**, that is he lays bare the transcendental onlooker in himself, he passes into him. This onlooker, however, does not first come to be by the **epoché**, but is only *freed* of the shrouding cover <barrier of anonymity> of human being [*Menschsein*].[32]

3. *Conversion*

The total phenomenological attitude and the **epoché** belonging to it are destined to effect, at first, a complete personal transformation, comparable in the beginning to a religious conversion, which then, however, over and above this, bears within itself the significance of the greatest existential transformation which is assigned as a task to mankind as such.[33]

For Husserl, the following is the continuity of steps that can achieve an intersubjective onlooker consciousness:

(a) producing an *epoché* by acts of *bracketing*;
(b) disclosing the atemporal *now* of *inward actuality* of self and/or other;
(c) directing (intending) reflection on the *epoché* toward being and the being of an other,[34] so that we are 'now living completely in such acts of the second degree';

(d) producing an *un-humanisation* in which we suspend positings of what is thought to be human;
(e) passing into the condition of *the transcendental onlooker*;
(f) entering into an *intersubjectivity* that (for Husserl) remains ego-centred;
(g) effecting, by all of the above, a *conversion* of our perception of being.

Although Husserl regarded 'intersubjectivity' as the pinnacle of human consciousness, most commentators agree that he never succeeded in explaining how it might be achieved and, correlatively, he never freed his idea of intersubjectivity from the one-sided control of the ego that he located in 'egological acts of empathy' and 'self-communalising'.[35] Among Shakespeare's representations, too, we will find failures to achieve intersubjectivity that are akin to Husserl's philosophical failure in this regard. Hamlet, I will argue, monumentalises one such failure. But, as we will also see, Shakespeare proceeded to achieve remarkable forms of intersubjectivity by working his way from comprehension of the grounds of Hamlet's failure.

For our concerns, it is well worth noting that Husserl's brilliant disciples, Fink and Alfred Schütz, not only attempted to comprehend the grounds of Husserl's failure to achieve intersubjectivity but to rectify it as well. They proceeded in a way that in effect offers precious insights into Shakespeare's own ultimate achievement of this kind. Fink and Schütz realised that the production of an *epoché* – even by each of two side-by-side subjectivities – was in itself insufficient for opening a space of the negative that could be shared by those subjectivities. The *epoché* produced by a given subjectivity *belongs* to the individual ego in that it is the place or locus of the emergence, beyond the stage of 'un-humanisation', of the actuality of that ego itself. Fink and Schütz therefore apply to the concept of a 'second *epoché*' that Husserl himself realised was needed here but failed to put to work in understanding how an intersubjectivity could be created. Fink's and Schütz's formulation of the 'second *epoché*' escapes the control of 'egological' consciousness and can help explain how Shakespeare finally overcomes ego-dominance in the chiasmata of theatricalisation and their first-order *epochés*. The escape from these things is achieved by a further mirror configuration of previously achieved mirrorings of self and other – precisely corresponding to Shakespeare's chiasmata of theatricalisation within the plays. This meta-configuration constitutes a chiastic 'object of reflection' that is beyond representation.[36] Contemplating this object of reflection can then produce a second-order *epoché* that is now completely detached from possession by anyone's ego.

What we experience in this second *epoché* are double self-cancellations of the *epoché* that was achieved by each subjectivity in its mirror chiasmus of self and projected imagining of the other, as well as – in the terms of a theatricalisation – of role-playing and would-be non-role-playing. The claims of the *solus ipse* are here dissolved into the radical negative space that is the location of no one's ego. To explain this complex, essential point, Schütz quoted Fink in full from a verbal exchange after Schütz's famous lecture on 'The Problem of Transcendental Intersubjectivity in Husserl':

> The experience of the Other involves a reciprocal relationship: in experiencing the Other concurrently I experience the Other's experiencing of me. But this reciprocal relationship is, taken strictly, not only a simple running back and forth from myself to the Other and from the Other to me. This reciprocal relationship allows, potentially, indefinite [i.e. infinite] reiteration. I can therefore say that I so experience the Other as the Other is experiencing me, and that the Other so experiences me as I am experiencing the Other . . . We have here an indefinite reciprocal reflectibility somewhat like two mirrors placed one opposite the other reflecting into each other in indefinite reiteration.[37]

The simultaneous and reciprocal double mirroring that Fink envisions here as an intersubjectivity corresponds to his description elsewhere of a second-order 'phenomenology of the phenomenological reduction', a 'making of the action of reduction the object of reflection'.[38] In an extrapolation from Kant's and Husserl's terms we can see that the effect of reflection on the object that is made from such double mirroring – that is of the previous *epoché*s of two subjectivities – is a second *epoché* that belongs to neither of the partnered subjectivities. I propose that, difficult as it may at first seem, this complex schema well describes Shakespeare's own achievement – intensely difficult as it, too, must initially seem. Shakespeare achieves his intersubjectivity with the spectator *from* and *outside* his paired plays. Thus, astonishingly enough, he achieves this by sharing, with the spectator, an object of directed chiastic reflection that is made from the mirroring of chiasmata *between* those plays.

The concrete intricacy of relation between the plays in each of these pairs of plays will be set out in detail in the pages that follow. Certainly, initially, it may be hard to believe that even Shakespeare could have produced a complexity of this order. Yet I believe that a careful demonstration of its workings will suggest that no hard thinking about Shakespeare's way of creating consciousness, at the peak of his career, can ignore this dimension of his labours. Coleridge claimed that the fictionality that inheres in all poetic representation requires a willing suspension of disbelief. What we experience in these plays of Shakespeare, however, is finally a carefully earned leap beyond such suspension of disbelief into experience that possesses immediate, unmediated credibility of a presentness that is beyond representation. Indeed, some readers will find it very difficult to believe that even Shakespeare could have been in possession of the extent of authorial forethought required for this degree of coordination between plays. With regard to such forethought, I suggest that the degree of credence required here is not that Shakespeare fully envisioned all the coordinated details of both partner plays, in each set, while already composing the first of them. Rather, we only need to imagine (admittedly this is no small thing) that in composing each play he was acutely aware of, and in the earlier play began to prime for later amendment, the inadequacies inherent in representational consciousness. At a certain moment – in composing *Hamlet* and *As You Like It*, I believe – he began to realise that such amendment could be provided by reflection on an extra-theatrical object created, formally not fictively, by side-by-side theatrical representations. Frank Kermode remarked of *The Winter's Tale* that 'we value it not for some hidden truth, but for its power to realize experience'.[39] My aim in these pages is to reconstruct the realised experience that is incrementally created by all of the plays discussed here and which in fact culminates in *The Winter's Tale*. Shared by playwright and spectator, this experience is of a species of consciousness that is beyond theatre per se.

Presentness and Spectatorship in King Lear: *from Cavell and Menke back to Husserl*

Since many readers will naturally think of parallel concerns in Cavell's brilliant essays in *Disowning Knowledge in Seven Plays of Shakespeare*, I wish to say another word about the different direction following Husserl – yet also prompted by Cavell's challenges – that my demonstrations take. The salient differences between Cavell's and Husserl's understandings of Cartesian scepticism emerge most clearly by considering Cavell's views of the spectatorship and presentness that are products, especially in *King Lear*, of that scepticism. Cavell writes:

> The perception or attitude demanded in following this drama [*King Lear*] is one which demands a continuous attention to what is happening at each here and now, as if everything of significance is happening at this moment, while each thing that happens turns a leaf of time. I think of it as an experience of *continuous presentness*. Its demands are as rigorous as those of any spiritual exercise . . .
>   Catharsis . . . is a matter of purging attachment from everything but the present, from pity for the past and terror of the future . . . What is revealed is my separateness from what is happening to [the protagonists of the tragedy and to fellow spectators]; that I am I, and here. It is only in this perception of them as separate from me that I make them present.[40]

The core of Cavell's views here has been illuminated by Christoph Menke's offer of an alternative to Cavell's account of presentness and spectatorship in *King Lear*. Menke builds his own account by expanding upon Nietzsche's perceptions of irony in *Hamlet*. In Menke's understanding of both *Hamlet* and *King Lear* the 'theatrical spectatorship' of the protagonist and the audience entails a 'doubly ironic reflection' that causes the 'dissolution of presentness' even in the 'experience of action'. The 'double irony' that Menke sees here is 'the (theatrical) irony of the player over against his role, which, according to his whims, he puts on or takes off like a mask' and 'the (dramatic) irony of fate, over against the agent's intentions, which themselves give rise to what turns against them'. Thus in Menke's view spectatorship in *King Lear*, as in *Hamlet*, interrupts 'absorption in the presentness of dramatic events and characters' by 'adhering to the rebukes of an irony that dissolves the dramatic present'.[41]

What seems to me most important here is that Cavell and Menke are both describing different stages of an experience of presentness that is embedded in a linear temporality.

Such a presentness continuously 'turns a leaf of time' (Cavell), while accompanying the 'experience of action' (Menke). Menke's recording of a 'dissolution of presentness' in 'theatrical spectatorship' can even be seen as a fulfilment of Cavell's description of the theatrical 'catharsis' that is the preliminary step of 'purging attachment from everything but the present'. Cavell's idea of a purged present, the demands of which are 'as rigorous as those of any spiritual exercise', requires a continuous attentiveness to worldly objects while that attentiveness is paradoxically detached from worldly impingements, detached as well, therefore, from the time of contingency in which pity and terror are occasioned. So, too, the picture of double irony that Menke observes in Shakespeare's spectatorship constitutes, on the concrete level of configured language, a four-way cancellation of polarities that has at least one important possibility that Menke has left out: in the very space or instant of the dissolution of chronological present time one might experience an inward presentness that is beyond the reach of time – that is wholly atemporal and that is detached from any linear temporality. For achieving this atemporal presentness, too, the initial movement, emphasised by Cavell, of alternately being with, and being separate from, others is certainly indispensable. For Husserl and, I believe, for Shakespeare as well, however, the inward presentness that is achieved in a momentary complete suspension of temporality is the key element that, only after that moment, enables us to return to the world and to others in that world.

Notes

1. Letter to George and Thomas Keats, 21 December 1817. Cited from *The Letters of John Keats, 1814–1821*, ed. Hyder E. Rollins, two vols (Cambridge, MA: Harvard University Press, 1958).

2. Letter to Benjamin Bailey, 22 November 1817.
3. Walter Jackson Bate, *John Keats* (Cambridge, MA: Harvard University Press, 1963), pp. 249–50. Bate's senior thesis at Harvard College, *Negative Capability: The Intuitive Approach in Keats*, was published by Harvard University Press in 1939.
4. Citations from the play are to the second quarto text used in *Hamlet*, ed. Ann Thompson and Neil Taylor (London: Bloomsbury, 2014).
5. Stanley Cavell, *Disowning Knowledge in Seven Plays of Shakespeare*, 2nd edn (Cambridge: Cambridge University Press, 2003), p. 190.
6. Stephen Greenblatt, 'The Death of Hamnet and the Making of Hamlet', *New York Review of Books* 21 October 2004. In slightly different forms these comments were incorporated into Greenblatt's *Will in the World: How Shakespeare Became Shakespeare* (New York: Random House, 2012). The phrase 'strange interim' echoes language in *Julius Caesar*.
7. Shakespeare's frequent use of the figure of chiasmus in his sonnets as well as his plays, including *Hamlet*, has been extensively documented. Joel Fineman, *Shakespeare's Perjured Eye: The Invention of Poetic Subjectivity in the Sonnets* (Los Angeles and Berkeley: University of California Press, 1986), explored chiasmus as the psychoanalytic master trope of Shakespeare's sonnets. Fineman briefly noted the devolution of ideas about chiasmus from Husserl's 'reduction and a transcendental ego' to Sartre and Merleau-Ponty to Lacan (p. 45). A sampling of the great extent of Shakespeare's use of chiasmus in the plays is available in articles by William L. Davis that also note earlier discussions of the subject: 'Better a Witty Fool than a Foolish Wit: The Art of Shakespeare's Chiasmus', *Text and Performance Quarterly* 23 (2003): 311–30 and 'Structural Secrets: Shakespeare's Complex Chiasmus', *Style* 39 (2005): 237–58. More recent is Chris Scholten-Smith's 'Some Chiastic Structures in Shakespeare's *Hamlet*', *Idiom* 46 (2010): 39–44.
8. Fascination with the perception of mirror reversal, from left to right, is already intense in antiquity. The same Plato who

provided, in the *Republic* (596c–e), the great precedent for Hamlet's idea of mimesis as a holding of a mirror up to nature also made explicit, in the *Timaeus* (section 1), the phenomenon of perceiving mirror reversal from left to right. See, among many others, Rebecca Bensen Cain, 'Plato on Mimesis and Mirrors', *Philosophy and Literature* 36.1 (2012): 187–95 and Tim Wilkinson, 'Mirror, Mirror', *Philosophy Now* 114 (2016) URL: <https://philosophynow.org/issues/114/Mirror_Mirror>. I am indebted to Stephen Hochstein for first pointing out to me this basic effect of all mirroring.

9. Lisa Freinkel, *Reading Shakespeare's Will: The Theology of Figure from Augustine to the Sonnets* (New York: Columbia University Press, 2002), pp. 22–3.

10. For 'Epistemological Reflections on Chiasmus' see *Chiasmus and Culture*, ed. Boris Wiseman and Anthony Paul (New York: Berghahn, 2014), pp. 91–140.

11. The first occurrence of the word 'now' in these lines is absent at this point in the second quarto but appears there in both the first quarto and the Folio.

12. I have discussed this aspect of the figure of apostrophe in *The Western Theory of Tradition: Terms and Paradigms of the Cultural Sublime* (New Haven: Yale University Press, 2000), pp. 71–88 and, specifically in relation to chiasmus, p. 90. I will later return to the topic of intentionality and chiasmus but I note already that David Woodruff Smith and Ronald Mcintyre, *Husserl and Intentionality: A Study of Mind, Meaning, and Language* (Dordrecht: Reidel, 1982) argue for the centrality of linguistic tensions of this kind – analogous, I believe, to those deployed in chiasmus – which they call 'intensionality': 'the intensionality of act-contexts is a manifestation in language of the conception of mental phenomena as intentional' (p. 33).

13. See Otto Schlapp, *Kants Lehre vom Genie, und die Entstehung der 'Kritik der Urteilskraft'* (Göttingen: Vandenhoeck & Ruprecht, 1901), p. 392.

14. Richard Eldridge, '"This Most Human Predicament": Cavell on Language, Intention, and Desire in Shakespeare', DOI: <https://doi.org/10.18192/cjcs.voi5.2414>, points out that

for Stanley Cavell, too, there is an experience of inhibition that produces a heightened experience of the self. Within scepticism this is an experience of alienation or estrangement from the demands and expectations of others that haunt ego formation.
15. I have traced Kant's encounters of the sublime in works of art in *Kant and Milton* (Cambridge, MA: Harvard University Press, 2010).
16. Freinkel, *Reading Shakespeare's Will*, p. 30.
17. Paul de Man, *Allegories of Reading: Figural Language in Rousseau, Nietzsche, Rilke, and Proust* (New Haven: Yale University Press, 1979), pp. 49–50.
18. The intentionality of chiasmus toward non-being has seemed inevitable to some theorists. In this vein, de Man's often quoted comments about chiasmus certainly do not have baleful intentions yet they are indicative of the chiastic consciousness formed on the intentionality toward – of building consciousness upon – non-being. De Man reads the nothing or negativity within chiasmus as a terminal *nihil*, a 'lack' within 'chiasmic' figuration that can only produce a misleading 'fiction' of continued life, a masking of language's incapacity to represent meaning. In that incapacity what is called 'death', he claims (correlatively at least), is no more than 'a displaced name for a linguistic predicament': see Paul de Man, *The Rhetoric of Romanticism* (New York: Columbia University Press, 1984), p. 81. De Man's location of a terminal void within chiasmus has been questioned on other grounds by Brian Vickers, 'Deconstruction's Designs on Rhetoric', in *Rhetoric as Pedagogy: Its History, Philosophy, and Practice – Essays in Honor of James J. Murphy*, ed. Winifred Bryan Horner and Michael Leff (London: Routledge, 1995), p. 304, and Frank B. Farrell, *Why Does Literature Matter?* (Ithaca: Cornell University Press, 2004), pp. 88– 90. I have commented on de Man's views of death within chiasmus and apostrophe in *The Western Theory of Tradition*, pp. 37–9, 92–6, 104–6. In the present Chapter 3, note 11 I return to de Man's claim.

19. It must be acknowledged at the outset that the precise mapping of the elements of chiasmata is often to some extent arbitrary, even if the experiential impact of the chiastic counter-movements of the elements – of sameness and difference – is undeniable. In other words, within chiastic structuring, the twistings and turnings back upon themselves of sameness and difference, as well as their effects (especially the resultant atemporal spaces of negativity), are inescapable.
20. On spectatorship in *King Lear* see, for example, Emily Sun, *Succeeding King Lear: Literature, Exposure, and the Possibility of Politics* (New York: Fordham University Press, 2010), pp. 62–72.
21. A. D. Nuttall, *Shakespeare the Thinker* (New Haven: Yale University Press, 2007), pp. 358–9.
22. I am here citing page 41 of Eugen Fink, *Sixth Cartesian Meditation: The Idea of a Transcendental Theory of Method*, trans. Ronald Bruzina (Bloomington: Indiana University Press, 1988), which was written in virtual partnership with Husserl, and Husserl, *Ideas Pertaining to a Pure Phenomenology and to a Phenomenological Philosophy: First Book: General Introduction to a Pure Phenomenology*, trans. F. Kersten (Dordrecht: Kluwer, 1998), § 50, p. 114. I return to these citations more fully below.
23. In a private communication Stephen Hochstein has suggested to me that Kent's phrases can be understood to describe something that is, at least in part, very similar in the modern physiology of vision, that is the way in which our reflexes of vision follow – from infancy onwards – someone else's gaze and look where they are looking.
24. See Jean-François Mattéi, 'The Heideggerian Chiasmus', in *Heidegger: From Metaphysics to Thought*, ed. Dominique Janicaud and Jean-François Mattéi, trans. Michael Gendre (Albany: SUNY Press, 1995), pp. 39–150; Merleau-Ponty, 'The Intertwining – The Chiasm', in *The Visible and the Invisible*, trans. Alphonso Lingis (Evanston: Northwestern University Press, 1968); Robin M. Muller, 'The Logic of the Chiasm in Merleau-Ponty's Early Philosophy', *Ergo* 4.7 (2017),

DOI: <http://dx.doi.org/10.3998/ergo.12405314.0004.00>; and Joel Smith, 'Merleau-Ponty and the Phenomenological Reduction', *Inquiry* 48.6 (2005): 553–7, which traces Merleau-Ponty's acceptance of the importance of the Husserlian *epoché*. In *The Visible and the Invisible*, pp. 248, 296, Merleau-Ponty explicates the workings of the chiasm, saying that what is invisible to consciousness is 'what in it prepares the vision of the rest . . . is what makes it see, is its tie to Being'. Rodolphe Gasché's 'Reading Chiasms', which is his introduction to Andrzej Warminski's *Readings in Interpretation: Hölderlin, Hegel, Heidegger* (Minneapolis: University of Minnesota Press, 1987), pp. ix–xxvi, surveys thinking about chiasmus in poststructuralism, especially in Paul de Man and Jacques Derrida. A variety of explorations of the relation of phenomenology to Shakespeare's thinking is offered in *Shakespeare and Phenomenology*, a special issue of *Criticism* 54.3 (2013), ed. Kevin Curran and James Kearney.

25. For discussion of the history and meaning of the term negativity see the introduction and essays in *Languages of the Unsayable: The Play of Negativity in Literature and Literary Theory*, ed. Sanford Budick and Wolfgang Iser (New York: Columbia University Press, 1989, reprinted Stanford: Stanford University Press, 1996). Jacques Derrida's essay in this volume discusses the *khôra* of Plato's *Timaeus*. I have commented on the negativity of the *khôra* of Sophocles's *Oedipus at Colonus* in 'The Emergence of Oedipus's Blessing: Evoking Wolfgang Iser', *Partial Answers* 7 (2009): 63–85.

26. See Husserl, 'Über die Reden Gotamo Buddhos', in *Der Piperbote für Kunst und Literatur* 2.1 (1925), pp. 18–19, now in *Husserliana: Edmund Husserl Gesammelte Werke*, XXVII, ed. Thomas Nenon and Hans Rainer Sepp (Dordrecht: Kluwer, 1989), pp. 125–6. Fred Hanna, 'Husserl on the Teachings of the Buddha', *Humanist Psychologist* 23 (1995): 365–72, includes an English translation of the essay. Hanna quotes Fink's assertion that 'the various phases of Buddhistic self-discipline were essentially phases of phenomenological reduction' (366). Beginning especially with Ramakant Sinari,

'The Method of Phenomenological Reduction and Yoga', *Philosophy East and West* 15 (1965): 217–28, there have been detailed explorations of the parallels between Husserl's phenomenological reduction and the Yoga Sutras. See also Husserl's 'Sokrates-Buddha: An Unpublished Manuscript from the Archives', ed. Sebastian Luft, in *Husserl Studies* 26.1 (2010): 1–17.

27. To the list offered above one should add, among many other things, that Heidegger and Sartre, and Husserl as well, were influenced by Kierkegaard's account of an 'anxiety of the nothing'. In the final phases of Husserl's thinking about phenomenology, he, too, became absorbed in Kierkegaard's writings, as Lev Shestov recounts, 'In Memory of a Great Philosopher: Edmund Husserl', trans. George L. Kline, <www.angelfire.com/nb/shestov/sar/husserl1.html>, section 1. For Kierkegaard's concept of the anxiety of the nothing, see *The Concept of Anxiety: A Simple Psychologically Orienting Deliberation on the Dogmatic Issue of Hereditary Sin*, trans. and ed. Reidar Thomte and Albert B. Anderson (Princeton: Princeton University Press, 1980), pp. 65, 96; cf. 41–6, 81–91. In my discussions below Kierkegaard's 'anxiety of the nothing' figures in a variety of ways.

28. The relevant discussion of Kant occurs in the *Critique of Pure Reason*, trans. Norman Kemp Smith (London: Macmillan, 1993), A 224–6, B 271–4 and is especially relevant to Husserl, in *Ideas: General Introduction to Pure Phenomenology*, trans. W. R. Boyce Gibson (New York: Collier, 1972), p. 107. Husserl's concept of the necessary directedness of consciousness is at least analogous to Kant's placement of the *a priori* categories of 'relation' (i.e. the categories of 'relation' in the Analogies of Experience: 'permanence', 'succession' and 'community of reciprocity'). In this instance I have cited Gibson's translation of *Ideas* rather than Kersten's (cited below) because the latter departs from Husserl's term 'actuality' (*Aktualität*), which (as has been frequently noted) recalls Kant's discussion of actuality (*Wirklichkeit*), although, as Ronald Bruzina points out in his translation and edition of Eugen Fink's *Sixth*

Cartesian Meditation, p. 196, n. cc, Husserl distinguishes what he means by *Aktualität* from what he means by *Wirklichkeit*. Bruzina explains that 'the condition of *Aktualität*, unlike *Wirklichkeit*, specifies (in Husserlian parlance) an actuality with the temporal character of the "now" – actuality in the *now*'. For Bruzina's parallel comment on Husserl's term '*aktuell*' in relation to the 'now' see p. lxvi.

29. Husserl, *Ideas Pertaining to a Pure Phenomenology and to a Phenomenological Philosophy*, § 50, p. 114. Here and in citations from Fink's *Sixth Cartesian Meditation*, angle brackets indicate Husserl's handwritten insertions.
30. Fink, *Sixth Cartesian Meditation*, p. 41. On pages 32–3, the idea of 'radical self-reflection' is elaborated together with Husserl's on-the-page notations.
31. Considering Husserl's omission of an acknowledgement of the debt of his *epoché* to Kant's '*Hemmung*' in the 'Analytic of the Sublime', it is hard to miss the profound resemblance between the point of view of Husserl's onlooker and the key value that Kant attributed to achieving a second, external point of view of 'community'. On Kant's second standpoint see Béatrice Longuenesse, *Kant on the Human Standpoint* (Cambridge: Cambridge University Press, 2005), especially pp. 184–208.
32. Fink, *Sixth Cartesian Meditation*, pp. 39–40.
33. Husserl, *Crisis of European Sciences and Transcendental Philosophy*, trans. David Carr (Evanston: Northwestern University Press, 1970), p. 137.
34. Despite the widespread acceptance of the importance of Husserl's insistence that consciousness of any object only takes place in an intention toward that object, there is a vast commentary on Husserl's vagueness about precisely what such intentionality is and what its relation to intersubjectivity might be. See, for example, Dan Zahavi, 'Husserl's Intersubjective Transformation of Transcendental Philosophy', in *The New Husserl: A Critical Reader*, ed. Donn Welton (Bloomington: Indiana University Press, 2003), p. 239, on the way Husserl's idea of 'intentionality is *a priori* dependent upon something,

which Husserl calls "open intersubjectivity"'. Dermot Moran, *Edmund Husserl: Founder of Phenomenology* (Cambridge: Polity Press, 2005), pp. 52–4, offers a clear overview of the matter and in his comments on Husserl's attempts at intersubjectivity makes this essential point: 'Husserl is paradoxical, insisting both on the genuineness of the experience of the other *as* other, and at the same time trying to locate all discussion methodologically in what he controversially calls the "sphere of ownness" (*Eigenheitssphäre*), "sphere of originality", or "primordial sphere" of myself, leading to the charge of solipsism' (p. 206).
35. Fink, *Sixth Cartesian Meditation*, p. 57.
36. The phrase 'object of reflection' is Fink's and is explained below.
37. Schütz, 'The Problem of Transcendental Intersubjectivity in Husserl (with Comments of Dorion Cairns and Eugen Fink)', trans. Fred Kersten, in *Schützian Research* 2 (2010): 47.
38. Fink, *Sixth Cartesian Meditation*, p. 48.
39. Frank Kermode, Introduction to *The Winter's Tale* (New York: New American Library, 1998), p. lxxvii.
40. Cavell, *Disowning Knowledge*, pp. 93, 109.
41. Menke, 'Tragedy and Skepticism: On *Hamlet*', in *Varieties of Skepticism: Essays after Kant, Wittgenstein, and Cavell*, ed. Andrea Kern and James Conant (Berlin: De Gruyter, 2014), pp. 377–83.

CHAPTER 2

'CONVERSION' OF THE 'NOTHING' BY THE INSTRUMENTALITY OF *THE MERCHANT OF VENICE*

As we have seen, Husserl believed that we can effect a moral 'conversion' in our thinking of the human by momentarily 'bracketing' consciousness and directing our achieved space of the negative – of the *epoché* – in a particular way. More than even that, Husserl was certain that conversion of this kind in consciousness was itself the first step towards gaining an authentic hold on actuality. Shakespeare anticipates and achieves all of these Husserlian steps – and more. We will now see how Shakespeare prepares the ground for his own way to such conversion, for himself and for the spectator. The story that goes beyond all story begins, or at least has one of its most significant beginnings, in *The Merchant of Venice*. There, in radical form, the inversive meanings of the 'nothing' begin to be glimpsed.

In *The Merchant of Venice* a variety of voices clamour for conversion.[1] The Christians loudly demand the Jew's conversion, while, as we will see, a fatalistic repetition of the 'three' – the magical term of *epistrophe* or conversion – eerily, proleptically, pervades the entire play, gesturing toward a conversion of an as yet unknown kind. The bogus conversion that is forced upon Shylock by Portia, as well as Portia's feeble announcement to Bassanio that 'what is mine, to you and yours / Is now converted' (3.2.152–67), only beckon with the false lights of prejudice and materialism. We are compelled to look elsewhere for what might constitute this conversion and what it might portend. I suggest that whatever this conversion may be, the precondition for achieving it, as for any genuine conversion, is attaining to a standpoint outside one's erstwhile consciousness, in this case, outside even the limits of the kinds of consciousness that are represented within this play. From that onlooking standpoint the playwright and the spectator of this play see that authentic conversion must most of all entail a transmutation in the meaning of the 'nothing' or space of the negative.

We do not need Husserl to see that *The Merchant of Venice* engages in a bracketing of its own kind by providing bookend representations of a thinking of the 'nothing'. These bookends are each so deeply problematic that their combined effect is to suggest the necessity of a viewpoint on the 'nothing' that could be maintained from a place outside the text. Opening the play, the first of these bookends is provided by Antonio's famously enigmatic words and Salarino's comment on them:

> ANTONIO: In sooth I know not why I am so sad.
> It wearies me, you say it wearies you;
> But how I caught it, found it, or came by it,
> What stuff 'tis made of, whereof it is born,
> I am to learn.[2]

Salarino claims that what makes Antonio 'so sad' is his fear that his three ships at sea will founder all at once and thus render him 'worth nothing' (1.1.36). Antonio rejects this explanation out of hand, and indeed his later responses to reports of material losses confirm that this is not the cause of his sadness. Yet Salarino has spoken more true than he knows. Shakespeare has planted a decisive clue to the aetiology of Antonio's malady in the suggestion that Antonio's so-called sadness is actually a deep anxiety of being 'worth nothing'. Salarino's business mind cannot begin to fathom the depth of that nothingness.

At the very close of Act 5, serving as the play's other bookend, we find Gratiano's insipid masculinist joke about potently satisfying his beloved's vaginal space of nothing: 'Well, while I live I'll fear *no other thing* [i.e. *nothing*] / So sore as keeping safe Nerissa's ring [*i.e. space of the nothing*]' (5.1.306–7). The narcissistic boasting and vaunted lust in Gratiano's final words certainly collapse his alleged care for his other into the egoistic space of self-satisfying desire. At the same time, the inner rhetorical workings of his protest of virility reveal the anxiety (the 'fear') of the nothing with which the play concludes. This is to say that a hidden anxiety of the sexualised nothing emerges within the infinite chiastic whirl of '[A] *no other thing* / [B] So sore as [B] keeping safe Nerissa's [A] ring'. Empty Gratiano's claim to a relationship between self and other thus corroborates and begins to explain (beyond Bassanio's understanding) Bassanio's early observation that 'Gratiano speaks an infinite deal of nothing, more than any man in all Venice' (1.1.114–15). An 'infinite deal' and of 'any *man*', indeed.[3] It would be an error to suppose that Shakespeare is here treating Gratiano's departing witticism with the same lightheadedness that Gratiano brings to it. To be sure, Shakespeare recurred frequently to this particular wordplay on the 'nothing'. F. H. Mares, referring most immediately to *Much Ado About Nothing*, notes that for Shakespeare '"nothing" as the "pudendal joke"' often 'grows to very serious issues indeed'.[4] I am proposing that the serious issue that Shakespeare attaches to the figuration of the 'nothing' is in this play at the core of the crisis of imagining *the being of being human*.

In trying to make sense of Antonio's fear of being 'worth nothing', Salarino adds these twisted phrases:

> shall I have the thought
> To think on this [i.e. being 'worth nothing'], and shall I lack the thought
> That such a thing bechanced would make me sad? (36–8)

The anxiety of being worth – deeply and completely – *nothing*, for which Antonio as well as Salarino have *no language*, is in Kierkegaard's terms the 'anxiety of the nothing' that is a 'dread' or '*Angst*' of totally losing one's sense of being, of floating in a hellish nothingness.[5] The weight of this seemingly weightless 'nothing' cannot be overestimated. To leap ahead to one of its most imposing occurrences in Shakespeare's plays, I again mention the instance of Kent's words to Lear on the excruciating subject of this nothingness. Having heard Cordelia's 'nothing' and seen its consequences, Kent says to Lear, 'let me still remain / The true blank of thine eye' (1.1.152–3). Shakespeare, we may say, sees eye to eye, blank to blank, with Kierkegaard in viewing the human condition as wedded to the permutations and perturbations of this blank nothingness.

Regarding one of those possible permutations, George Pattison usefully remarked that Kierkegaard's 'anxiety of the nothing' can amount to an 'anxious sublime' that is closely related to Kant's terms for the sublime in the third *Critique*. Pattison suggested that the possibility of this 'Kierkegaardian sublime' with its Kantian dimensions is 'disclosed in the discovery of the enormity of inwardness that is the obverse of the enormity of vacuity'.[6] I am proposing that Shakespeare's 'nothing' in *The Merchant of Venice* stands ready to be converted from enormity of vacuity to enormity of inwardness, and even of an intersubjective sharing of inwardness. Yet the act of this conversion requires an Archimedean leverage that can only be applied from outside the play. Only the playwright and spectator, not the play's protagonists, can achieve that extra-theatrical standpoint. We will see in Chapter 4 that, in this case, that standpoint will not be fully achieved until Shakespeare – having learned how to place *Hamlet* and *As You Like It* side by side – places *Othello* side by side with *The Merchant of Venice*.

Within *The Merchant of Venice*, the vacuity of the nothing can certainly seem to reign supreme. While some readers have steadfastly fixed their gaze on the play's fairytale features of apparently plenitudinous perfection, many commentators have noted the degraded values for which the play's apparent heroes stand. Their claims for Christian mercy are repeatedly belied by the merciless legalism and unabashed greed that accompany and express their Jew-hatred. Shylock's hatred of Christians and his own merciless legalism and unabashed greed are mirror images of the Christians' behaviour. At the very least, a reactive, distanced reflection on this surface drama is thus an inner necessity generated by the play itself.[7] I will later demonstrate how, in fact, Shakespeare here begins to project a counter-life of language that the playwright and the spectator can finally access together. This he begins to achieve in *The Merchant of Venice* itself by casting a net of shadow meanings for a linkage of the play's key terms, namely *nothing*, *hazard*, *three* or the *third*, and *conversion*. These suggestive bifurcations of some meanings do not amount to subversion of all meanings, such as a deconstructionist reading might aim to uncover. From the beginning to the ending of this play – to an ultimate ending that is beyond the play – the instrumentality of this play step by step prepares for a language of self-reflection. This language will express, for the playwright and spectator, fully stable meanings of the nothing.

Within the play, Shakespeare plumbs the anxiety of the nothing to an archetypal depth. At that depth the warranty of the self always seems, at first, to be purchased at the cost of the being of the other. The two can wax and wane inversely in a horrifying symmetry – made intensely horrifying in this play because the blessing of being is here claimed as election by a divine agent who has now abandoned his initial choice for elected being. At the centre of experience of this inversive, chiastic round emerges a 'nothing' that, directed with annihilating force, only confirms the anxiety of the nothing that self and other equally suffer. Shakespeare mercilessly cuts through the pieties of any easy deferring between self and other. He recognises that in order to exit this circle of soul-deep rivalry a standpoint outside these mutually deficiting interchanges must somehow be achieved. No one in the play achieves that standpoint.

Two Kinds of 'Nothing'

Although *nothing* is in itself invariable (zero, a cipher), how it is framed determines very different thoughts of the nothing. Within *The Merchant of Venice*, we encounter, almost exclusively, only the 'nothing' of monetary or sexual pretence to a worldly fullness that merely conceals utter emptiness. Belmont, with its fabulous affluence and redolent sexuality, is a fantasy playground in which momentary gestures of self-effacement, such as Bassanio or Antonio or Portia offer, cannot long disrupt this company's certainty of guaranteed gratifications. Gratiano's final words would ratify the impression that Bel-mont is a *mons veneris*, a locus of perpetual sexual friction in the allegedly 'real' world of this 'nothing'. This same Gratiano loudly demands Shylock's total annihilation in the loop or ring of the hangman's noose: 'A halter gratis – *nothing* else, for God's sake' (4.1.375; emphasis added). The invocation of 'God's sake' is telling here, even if Gratiano hardly understands the theological vibrations he is here inciting. Also in the vein of theological polemics, Portia issues words of nullifying 'justice' in what Stanley Cavell calls her 'mock Talmudism'.[8] She thus fulfils the annihilation of Shylock into the 'nothing' that Gratiano demands. She claims to act as if 'for God's sake' by casting away – or pretending to convert – 'the Jew', not least because he has repeatedly implied his people's priority and legalism of 'God's sake':

> The Jew shall have all justice . . .
> He shall have *nothing* but the penalty . . .
> Thou [Shylock] shalt have *nothing* but the forfeiture,
> To be so taken at thy peril, Jew. (4.1.317–18, 439–40; emphases added)

Bassanio may seem to distance himself from Gratiano's 'infinite deal of nothing', yet he is himself deeply immersed in the pure materialism of that emptiness. To Portia, he laments his worldly nothingness in a way that demonstrates an incapacity to imagine a nothing that is not money-determined:

> dear Lady,
> Rating myself at *nothing*, you shall see
> How much I was a braggart. When I told you
> My state was *nothing*, I should have told you
> That I was worse than *nothing*. (3.2.255–9; emphases added)

Through its own instrumentality, reaching beyond itself, *The Merchant of Venice* begins to generate the necessity of the other kind of nothing that is a beginning of the human. This nothing is at the heart of acceptance of our own potential nothingness and concomitant suspension of accustomed ideas of the human. In Husserl's terms, this must be an '*Entmenschung*', an 'un-humanisation'. This kind of nothing is only locatable in the risk that Shakespeare incurs – hazards – by creating the play itself.

'Hazard'

Shakespeare here coordinates the language of becoming or being 'nothing' with the language of being at 'hazard' to reduction to that 'nothing'. In *The Merchant of Venice* everyone faces acute hazard of one kind or another. With regard to the dramatis personae this is repeatedly made obvious. Bassanio is the first to speak of the 'hazard' of his dubious fortunes, which he is too dimly aware could also entail Antonio's own hazard (1.1.139–51). So, too, Portia's destiny, her very person, are locked into the whims of a silly game. Of course, all the hangers-on to Bassanio's and Portia's fortunes are subject to the same or similar hazards, while Jessica throws herself upon the mercies of a Christian lover who, as has been pointed out, by Venetian law, can never confer Christian status upon her.[9] Needless to say, hazard hovers throughout over the head of Shylock.

We may not at first see Shakespeare's own hazard in producing the text and the performance of this play, yet it is actually far more perilous than any suffered by the characters within his play. And it is Shakespeare's hazard that projects the deeper hazard that all the individuals in Shakespeare's audience individually face in viewing *The Merchant of Venice*. No matter how insistently we suspend disbelief in the fictionality of the dramatis personae, we know, on some level, that their hazard is fictive. Shakespeare's hazard is a function of the fictive yet it remains for him and for his audience – on the level of his contemporary world – alive and glaring after this play is concluded. Shakespeare's representation of Shylock eschews the reductionism of the Pantalone of Commedia dell'arte or the comic devil of the morality plays. Yet by painting Shylock with devilish colours while also bestowing upon him unmistakable, even grand, dimensions of humanity, Shakespeare has plunged his play into a moral dilemma from which there is no exit, at least not within the play. *The Merchant of Venice* commits the imaginary erasure of a human being, allegedly for the sake of the moral imagination.

Even if we are not members of Shylock's 'tribe' (3.1.61) we cannot fail to hear that in *The Merchant of Venice* the word Jew is consistently charged with obliterative violence. Ranged as a choric team against Shylock, the other characters of the play repeatedly spit out the Jew-word upon him as a fierce execration, as if inspired by the way Antonio 'did void' his 'rheum' upon Shylock's Jewish 'beard' (1.1.109). As even the briefest survey of the word's occurrences in the play shows, the Jew malediction explodes from an atavistic, affricative *J*, as if prior to formed language, against an object that, most of the time, does not rate an individual's name.[10] Shakespeare's representation of the total muting of Shylock is itself shockingly muted. Once effected, this act of muting itself vanishes suddenly and totally, without a later trace or vibration to tell us where it occurred. Knowingly but beyond his full control, Shakespeare has here put his moral consciousness – his humanity or human empathy – at acute hazard. Yet, as I have begun to suggest, although Shakespeare cannot directly avoid participation in this pathology, he poises himself for leaping over it in a reflection on the play's own vast emptinesses and nullifications. At the very least, this irresolvable clash of values has the effect of suspending judgement concerning what the human is. In addition, Shakespeare avails himself of other powerful resources for effecting this suspension and, ultimately, for newly disclosing his – and the spectator's – empathy with being.

The 'Third' of Conversion

Throughout the *Merchant of Venice* Shakespeare engages these rival siblings (Christian and Jew) in a game of hazard that climaxes in the number *three* and its variants, the *third*, *thrice* and *treble*. This number or numbering, including doubling and trebling of three, is heard like a drumbeat – in fact, more than three dozen times – throughout the play. The game of the three is outwardly played with reference to two specific themes: the game of hazard that risks reduction to the worldly nothing and the drive to convert the Jew.[11] In the worldly game played by Bassanio, Portia and their cohorts the winning number is imagined to be three. Yet in the rules of the dicing game called 'hazard' the caster of the number three in fact 'casts out' of the game.[12] In *The Merchant of Venice* the vaunted successes of the third suitor, Bassanio, for the 'third' casket (2.7.8) and of Antonio's gamble at sea with his 'three' argosies (5.1.276) are in fact unsuccessful concealments of the frantic superficiality – the rounds of fortune-hunting emptiness – of their daily pursuits. Far from having Trinitarian associations, for the Christian gamblers in this play, the three and the third are the high stakes for winning everything financial, legal and sexual on the table. If we could read the *The Merchant of Venice*, restrictively, as pure comedy, none of this would be problematic. That, however, is here impossible. These gamesters cast their hazard throws on the life-and-death gamble that must result in either Antonio's death or Shylock's annihilative 'conversion'. This annihilation is no mere temporary confinement of a Malvolio to a dark room. In a difficult but strongly felt sense, these gamblers, and even the play as a whole, have 'cast out' to a realm of meaningless triviality. At the same time, a meaningful attainment to conversion of the 'nothing' continuously fails to emerge, at least not in the play itself. Yet access to an unworldly conversion is opened by another lexical field of meanings that is appended to that *casting out*.

In the footsteps of other scholars, Michel Foucault explained that, historically and philosophically considered, the third 'turn' or *epistrophe* is far more than a figure of rhetoric. *Epistrophe* is the fulfilling third stage of *conversion* in the triple pattern of the original (*mone*), emergence (*prodos*) and conversion (*epistrophe*) that was taken up from Plato's term for the object of education – '*epistrophe*'. *Epistrophe*, the 'turning around of the soul' (*Republic*, 7.521c) – was given new life in Neoplatonism and early Christianity.[13] In *The Merchant of Venice* the conversion of Shylock that is demanded by the Christians would, they imagine, be the legitimation of all their desires. In Shylock's hypnotic echoing of the terms of 'three' in the drawing up of the bond we hear the doom of an unwitting prophecy of the moment when he, not Antonio, will be 'bound' – bound, that is, to a total loss of will, to disintegration into what the Christians will call conversion: 'Three thousand ducats, well . . . for three months . . . for three months, well . . . Three thousand ducats for three months, and Antonio bound' (1.3.1–9). After Jessica has absconded and Shylock is being mocked by Salarino, Shylock impotently repeats this tripling again and again, saying of Antonio, 'Let him look to his bond . . . let him look to his bond . . . let him look to his bond' (3.1.37–9). Soon after, Shylock will cry to the jailer three times, 'I'll have my bond . . . my bond . . . my bond' (3.3.4–5). Shylock is self-trapped by the three. The ostensibly prophetic fulfilment of the three, not in Antonio's bond but in Shylock's acceptance of conversion, seems inevitable. Conversion, *epistrophe* of the third, will be forced from him exactly in the measure of his bond of three's. Or so it seems.

Shakespeare has in fact earlier hinted that the way to conversion in this play, a way that will presumably culminate in Shylock's conversion, is not as smooth as it may seem. We recall that thrice-lucky Bassanio addresses Portia as 'thrice-fair lady' and asks that she triply seal – *confirm, sign and ratify* – his success:

> stand I even so,
> As doubtful whether what I see be true,
> Until confirmed, signed, and ratified by you. (3.2.146–8)

Portia, who will be the instrument of Shylock's forced 'conversion', takes up the game of the apparently winning, worldly three and extends it by trivialising it down to its common lowest denomination, that is as mere currency 'conversion'. Here I again cite her response to Bassanio, this time with a deeper awareness of the portents of the inwoven treble or three, 'for you / I would be trebled twenty times myself; . . . what is mine, to you and yours / Is now converted' (3.2.152–67). Throughout the play, these three's hint at the possibility of a spiritual conversion that continually recedes and finally disappears, dissolved in the giddy partying that ends the play.

Husserl's 'Reduction' and Kant's 'Deduction' in the Sublime

Here I return to Pattison's suggestion that the potentiality of a Kantian deduction of an 'anxious sublime' is implicit in the 'anxiety of the nothing'. We can explain how this suggestion can be made good in practice by again noting that in Kantian terms activating this potentiality entails the suspension of consciousness of the external world by trying, and failing, to grasp the totality of an effectively endless progression of items in the field of consciousness (5:250). In encounters with works of sublime art, at least, the mind thus actively brackets consciousness of the world, producing in this 'deduction' the 'inhibition' – the '*Hemmung*' – of consciousness that is very like the '*epoché*' or 'withholding' in Husserl's 'reduction'. Kant's and Husserl's ideas of cognitive disinterestedness arguably diverge in a variety of ways. Yet both locate a moment of disinterestedness that suspends worldly spatiotemporality. The residual self abides there in a negativity that is its own atemporality.

Anticipating the power of Kant's and Husserl's insights, Shakespeare develops his own arsenal of ways to begin to achieve a reduction to the transcendental 'nothing'. As we have seen, in *The Merchant of Venice* the repetition of the empty 'nothing' sets in motion a progression of the kind that experience of the Kantian sublime requires. In addition, as I began to note earlier, within *The Merchant of Venice* a key instrument of Shakespeare's reduction toward the 'nothing' is his deployment of chiasmus. The following are exemplary chiasmata in the play's annihilating cross-movements of self and other:

SHYLOCK: [A] *The villainy you teach me* [B] I will *execute*, and [B] *it shall go hard* but I will better [A] *the instruction*. (3.1.53–7; emphases added)

PORTIA: [A] *Thou* [Shylock] [B] *shalt have nothing but the forfeiture*,
[B] *To be so taken at thy peril*, [A] *Jew*. (4.1.317–18; emphases added)

In the following example, Portia even coerces Shylock into cooperation in a chiasmus of his own self-nullification, centred in the nothing:

PORTIA: [A] Art thou *contented*, [B] *Jew*? What dost thou say?
SHYLOCK: [B] *I* [A] am *content*. (4.1.389–90; emphases added)

This intentionality of the *epoché* and the nothing that is directed *toward non-being* is the dehumanising staple of this play. As we will see later, only the playwright and the spectator together can convert the intentionality *toward non-being* into an intentionality that is directed *towards being*. In the present case, this will only take place when the playwright and spectator achieve the status of onlookers to this play *together* with *Othello*.

Towards the Extra-theatrical Condition of the Onlooker in The Merchant of Venice

The movement toward the status of onlookers not *in* but *by The Merchant of Venice*, which is to say only in partnership with *Othello*, will become the key to understanding what Shakespeare came to envision as the two plays' joint achievement. In *The Merchant of Venice* itself the spectator already experiences intimations of the necessity for this extra-theatrical fulfilment. This occurs in the moments when a space of interruption or the negative is opened by acute *suspensions of suspensions of disbelief* within the represented fiction or story. To some extent this is achieved in out-of-place topical references such as the mention of the very recent shipwrecks on the Goodwins (3.1.3). Two, more decisive exits from the play's fictional space take place in the conclusion of the trial scene. After Shylock has wordlessly acquiesced to Antonio's demand to 'presently become a Christian' (4.1.383) and says his last words (ever), the Duke says 'Get thee gone' while Gratiano jeers:

> In christening shalt thou have two godfathers:
> Had I been judge, thou shouldst have had ten more,
> To bring thee to the gallows, not to the font. (4.1.393–6)

M. M. Mahood cannily notes the way these verses break 'theatrical illusion', yet even so she misses the vital effect and role of this breaking of illusion. Mahood writes:

> The English-sounding joke about trial by jury [i.e. the then familiar joke that twelve so-called 'godfathers' send a condemned man to God's judgment] deliberately snaps the theatrical illusion as Gratiano . . . makes use of a Fool's liberty to step out of a play and ally himself with its audience. For a dramatist to switch off one of his most brilliant illusions is an act of bravado, a way of celebrating the success with

which he has compelled the audience to suspend all disbelief in what it has witnessed.[14]

We need to wonder, however, what this alliance between Gratiano and Shakespeare's audience – very much outside the play – amounts to. From this alliance, he and they step out of the play and re-enter it only to break, to suspend, the suspension of disbelief in the play's fictionality. As Mahood notes, Gratiano is certainly playing on his English audience's well-developed interest in what goes on in English court trials. Yet to break in here so fully, at this critical moment, he needs to play on much more than that. Ironically enough, despite Gratiano's fervid efforts to erase Shylock from the world, Shylock's so-called conversion powerfully cooperates with Gratiano in breaking the suspension of disbelief in the play's fictionality.

Shakespeare has prepared the moment of Shylock's abrupt and allegedly sincere conversion to make it totally unbelievable. No reader or spectator can believe or bear witness, with hand on heart, that the mind of this spat-upon spokesperson for the suffering of the Jews at the hands of Christians can freely embrace even a shred of sincere belief in the Christian system of dogma and violent power that persecutes him. Of course, Shylock's whole-hearted belief of this kind is precisely what would be required to allow anyone to believe in this 'conversion'. Here the theatrical illusion has already been shattered irreversibly. When Shylock abruptly leaves the stage he takes with him our credence in the fiction that has represented him. The spectator is here left in the lurch, in an empty, negative space, by this additional breaking or suspension of illusion in this play.

The Einbruch *of Anti-Semitism*

In *The Merchant of Venice* the chief hazard of bracketing the human is by Shakespeare purposively made to occur in the intrusion, en bloc, of Christian Jew-hatred directly from Shakespeare's own place and time into the space and time of the play. To be sure, this Christian anti-Semitism or Jew-hatred claimed the existence of a symmetrical (albeit powerless) Jewish hatred of Christians, such as Shylock expresses toward Antonio in his one aside in the play: 'I hate him for he is a Christian' (1.3.34).

To describe the effect of the intrusion of anti-Semitism in *The Merchant of Venice* I cite – and amend – Carl Schmitt's concept of an 'intrusion of the time', an '*Einbruch*' or 'breaking-in', of an extra-fictional reality into the reality represented on stage. Schmitt argues that in *Hamlet* Shakespeare exploits his contemporary audience's anxiety concerning a contemporary crisis of succession and election to produce a powerful effect: 'historical time breaks into [*einbricht*] the time of the play' to create a space of rupture within the temporality of the theatrical fiction.[15] Considering Schmitt's own earlier dissemination of extreme anti-Semitic beliefs as a member of the Nazi party, it is ironic but perhaps not surprising that even with his insight into the *Einbruch* of an anxiety of monarchical election in *Hamlet*, he apparently did not see the even more powerful *Einbruch* of the *ur*-anxiety of all elections in Judaeo-Christian cultures. This is the anxiety of theological election that underpins the anti-Semitism of *The Merchant of Venice*. Here the anxiety of theological election attaches itself to the anxiety of the nothing. The Abraham of the book of Genesis was the first to embrace divine election – to divinely blessed being – for the Jews. Even though Abraham is from the first told by the Lord that the blessing he carries will be a blessing to 'all the families of the earth' (Gen. 12: 3), the Jewish priority of this divine election continuously created vast anxiety for the Christianity that claimed to replace Judaism. Saint Paul repeatedly addressed and mediated this anxiety, which for many Christians nevertheless remained as deep as the hold on being itself.

Julia Lupton and Jennifer Rust explain that for Schmitt the importance of the *Einbruch* into the temporality of the theatrical fiction is that it shows that 'the play space of *Hamlet* always remains open to the negative space of historical trauma'.[16] Schmitt's argument for such an '*Einbruch*' in *Hamlet* is certainly insightful. Yet his claim for a language of inherent political violence in the art of *Hamlet* presents a distorted picture of the fit of form and content in that art. As I will explain in Chapter 3, in my view the overarching artistic problematic of *Hamlet* is how to overcome the prison of theatricalisation in which Hamlet's question about the player, 'What's Hecuba to him, or he to her . . . ?' is central. As already noted in Chapter 1, the chiastic form of Hamlet's question, or outcry, moves on the polarities of *play-acting* to *would-be non-play-acting / would-be non-play-acting* to *play-acting*. Many have noted that Schmitt's conception of the 'real' history that intrudes into *Hamlet* is naive in a way that Shakespeare, of all the world's great dramatists, would have found most impossible to take at face value.[17] For Shakespeare the 'real' of the so-called real world is also formed on play-acting, so that the play-acting of theatre and the play-acting outside theatre invade each other. For Shakespeare every *breaking-in* or *Einbruch* of the time of the outer world into a play always oscillates, back and forth, with the potentiality of a *breaking-out*, an *Ausbruch* (indeed, as from a prison) out of the play. The effect of this chiastic oscillation – of *Einbruch* to *Ausbruch / Ausbruch* to *Einbruch* – can itself be to begin to produce a shared *epoché* in which playwright and spectator stand as onlookers from outside the play, in this case outside *The Merchant of Venice*.

Although Schmitt did not acknowledge it, it is decidedly not accidental that the effect of the *Einbruch* which he describes, closely, and not accidentally, resembles Husserl's *epoché* and its power of illuminating Shakespeare's art. Schmitt was well aware that his concept of an *Einbruch* that produces a temporal rupture is itself a version of Walter Benjamin's engine of 'blasting' open a free '*Jetztzeit*' (in his 'Theses on the Philosophy of History') which, as Benjamin was himself well aware, is in turn a version of Husserl's *epoché* and 'blasting open' of the *now*.[18] In the case of *The Merchant of Venice* this philosophical genealogy helps us grasp more clearly the manifestations and meanings of the reduction and *epoché* in the *Einbruch* of anti-Semitism. Shakespeare doubles the *Einbruch* chiastically, back and forth, with the *Ausbruch* to his audience. The rotating chiasm of *Einbruch / Ausbruch // Ausbruch / Einbruch* begins to generate the negative space of Shakespearean onlooker consciousness. The minds of the spectator and playwright, as onlookers directed towards each other, are each here endlessly confronted with their failure to grasp the totality of that progression. The product of this chiastic movement is the space of the negative that is now converted into an un-worldly nothing directed toward the being of the other. Yet Shakespeare saw the need to create a higher-order suspension of chiasmus if the conversion of the nothing was to be brought to fulfilment. We will see that, supplementary to the extra-theatrical chiastic effect of this *Einbruch / Ausbruch // Ausbruch / Einbruch* in *The Merchant of Venice*, the onlooker playwright and onlooker spectator can go on to experience a second *epoché*, a conversion to an unworldly nothing. This takes place in the construction of a chiastic object of reflection between this play as a whole with another play – *Othello* – also as a whole.

Shakespeare came to realise, that is, that the full experience and intentionality of a second *epoché* toward being could only be achieved extra-theatrically by the playwright and the spectator who reflect on the form created by the chiastic relations of two plays together. Shakespeare had not yet come to this full realisation, much less found the means of its effectuation, at the time of composing *The Merchant of Venice*. I therefore ask for the reader's patience with an abeyance in my discussion of *The Merchant of Venice*. Before opening discussion of the partnering of *The Merchant of Venice* with *Othello*, I will proceed to show that Shakespeare first achieved a large-scale envisioning of these extra-theatrical problems and their solution – their production of a kind of consciousness that is projected beyond theatricalisation – in *Hamlet* and its partnered relation to *As You Like It*. After discussing these gains in *Hamlet* and *As You Like It*, I will demonstrate Shakespeare's further advance in turning back, epicyclically, to *The Merchant of Venice* in order to create a highly similar chiastic partnership with *Othello*. After that, the way will be open to considering the crowning of all these increments of consciousness in the partnering of *King Lear* and *The Winter's Tale*.

Notes

1. One of the starting points for my thinking about *The Merchant of Venice* was Julia Reinhard Lupton's 'Exegesis, Mimesis, and the Future of Humanism in *The Merchant of Venice*', *Religion and Literature* 32 (2000): 123–39.
2. Citations from the play are to *The Merchant of Venice*, ed. M. M. Mahood (Cambridge: Cambridge University Press, 2003), which with few exceptions follows the first quarto.
3. It has sometimes been suggested that the blockage and repression of Antonio's homoerotic desire for Bassanio is related to his sadness. Viewed as an ancillary, intensifying factor, this makes sense. Yet, given the web of motivations that this play traces and given Shakespeare's broad tolerance for erotic desire of various kinds, it is difficult to believe that he was here representing blocked homoerotic desire as the source of all the play's complications.
4. F. H. Mares (ed.), Shakespeare, *Much Ado About Nothing* (Cambridge: Cambridge University Press, 2003), pp. 33–4.
5. For Kierkegaard's concept of the 'anxiety of the nothing', see *The Concept of Anxiety: A Simple Psychologically Orienting*

Deliberation on the Dogmatic Issue of Hereditary Sin, trans. and ed. Reidar Thomte and Albert B. Anderson (Princeton: Princeton University Press, 1980), pp. 65, 96; cf. 41–6, 81–91. For Kant's language of the sublime see especially the *Critique of the Power of Judgment*, trans. Paul Guyer and Eric Matthews (Cambridge: Cambridge University Press, 2000), 5: 245, 258, 265, 313, 318. If Kierkegaard's ideas remind us of what seem to be similar ideas in Heidegger's formulations of 'What Is Called Thinking' or 'The End of Philosophy and the Task of Thinking' that is at least in part because of the impact of Kierkegaard, as well as Kant, on Heidegger. We may add here that the Kantian criterion for moral thought of a totally inclusive community of being in reciprocity (as in the categorical imperative and Kingdom of Ends of the *Groundwork* or discussions in the *Opus postumum*) is for Kant (and for Shakespeare's *beyond* as well) a possible defence against Alasdair MacIntyre's criticism of Kierkegaard for advocating a 'criterionless choice': see *After Virtue: A Study in Moral Theory*, 2nd edn (South Bend: University of Notre Dame Press, 1984), p. 39. For a variety of responses to MacIntyre's criticisms of Kierkegaard see *Kierkegaard after MacIntyre: Essays on Freedom, Narrative, and Virtue*, ed. John Davenport and Anthony Rudd (Chicago: Open Court, 2001).

6. George Pattison, 'Kierkegaard and the Sublime', *Kierkegaard Studies Yearbook* 3 (1998): 245–75. The cited sentence is from page 274.

7. The widely divergent responses that constitute the history of reception of *The Merchant of Venice* turn precisely on whether one recognises that inner necessity. A. D. Nuttall, *A New Mimesis: Shakespeare and the Representation of Reality* (New Haven: Yale University Press, 2007; first published 1983), pp. 130–1, puts his finger directly on this question – 'the most difficult point', he calls it – and decides against the recognition. Nuttall's comments on the play in *Shakespeare the Thinker* (New Haven: Yale University Press, 2007), especially pp. 255–62, enrich and somewhat qualify his earlier reading though he still largely accepts the mercifulness of the

Christians' forgiveness of Shylock and he still cannot see the possibility of the play's non-subversive counter-thesis.
8. Stanley Cavell, 'Saying in *The Merchant of Venice*', in *Shakespeare and the Law: A Conversation among the Disciplines*, ed. Bradin Cormack, Martha C. Nussbaum and Richard Strier (Chicago: University of Chicago Press, 2013), p. 223.
9. See Janet Adelman, *Blood Relations: Christian and Jew in The Merchant of Venice* (Chicago: University of Chicago Press, 2008), p. 163, n. 10.
10. For example, those at 2.8. 4, 3.1.17–18, 3.2.296, 3.2.315–16, 4.1.112, 4.1.283–8, 4.1.343–4.
11. This kind of numbers game is certainly not unique to *The Merchant of Venice*. Shakespeare extensively plays such a game with the number three, for example in *Julius Caesar* where the number is a deeply ominous portent. Shakespeare's interest in the game of hazard – the most popular dicing game in Europe throughout the late Middle Ages and the Renaissance – was already evidenced in *Richard III* where the number three is suggestively linked to a fateful cast of the dice, indeed in a sudden-death roll of the number three. While repeating an epistrophic triplication – 'A horse! A horse! My kingdom for a horse!' – Richard declares, 'I have set my life upon a cast, / And I will stand the hazard of the die' (5.7.7–13). Even a partial list of the occurrences of three and its variants (including explicit multiples) in *The Merchant of Venice* would include those at the following lines: 1.3.1, 2, 3, 8 (twice), 16, 21, 48, 66 (twice), 95, 96, 114, 152 ('thrice three times'); 2.7.8, 48; 3.1.61; 3.2.146, 153, 297, 298, 299; 4.1.42, 84, 85, 223, 230, 407; 5.1.276.
12. For the rules of hazard, which remained more or less stable well into the nineteenth century, see pp. 170–1 of Rhiannon Purdie, 'Dice-games and the Blasphemy of Prediction', in *Medieval Futures: Attitudes to the Future in the Middle Ages*, ed. John Anthony Burrow and Ian P. Wei (Woodbridge, Suffolk: Boydell Press, 2000), pp. 167–84. One indication of the popularity of the game of hazard is Chaucer's mention of it, twelve times, in 'The Pardoner's Tale'.

13. For the importance of *epistrophe* in Foucault's thinking see Edward F. McGushin, *Foucault's Askesis: An Introduction to the Philosophical Life* (Evanston: Northwestern University Press, 2007), pp. 110–14. Foucault was especially influenced here by Paul Aubin, *Le problème de la 'conversion'* (Paris: Beauchesne, 1963) and Pierre Hadot, *Exercices spirituels et philosophie antique*, 2nd edn (Paris: Albin, 2000). *Epistrophe* was already treated extensively by Arthur Darby Nock in *Conversion: The Old and the New in Religion from Alexander the Great to Augustine of Hippo* (Baltimore: Johns Hopkins University Press, 1998; first published by Oxford University Press, 1933).
14. *The Merchant of Venice*, ed. Mahood, p. 16. So, too, as Mahood notes, in Shylock's address to the Duke, his references to 'your charter and your city's freedom' (4.1.38–9) cannot refer to Venice but describe, instead, the privileges granted to an English city by a feudal monarch.
15. Carl Schmitt, *Hamlet or Hecuba: The Intrusion of the Time into the Play*, trans. David Pan and Jennifer R. Rust, intro. Jennifer R. Rust and Julia Reinhard Lupton (Candor, NY: Telos Press, 2009), p. 44. Schmitt's German title was *Hamlet oder Hekuba: Der Einbruch der Zeit in das Spiel*.
16. *Hamlet or Hecuba*, p. 1.
17. See Rust and Lupton's introduction to *Hamlet or Hecuba*, p. xxvii, for discussions of Schmitt's 'real'.
18. On Benjamin's relation to Husserl see Uwe Steiner. 'Phänomenologie der Moderne: Benjamin und Husserl', *Benjamin-Studien* 1 (2008): 107–25, as well as comments by Peter Fenves throughout *The Messianic Reduction: Walter Benjamin and the Shape of Time* (Stanford: Stanford University Press, 2011), and by Sami Khatib, 'A Non–Nullified Nothingness: Walter Benjamin and the Messianic', *Stasis* 1 (2013): 82–108.

CHAPTER 3

TOWARDS AN ESCAPE FROM THEATRICALISATION: *HAMLET* AND *AS YOU LIKE IT*

In the six plays that are our concern here, Shakespeare again and again escaped theatricalisation by creating a totally non-representational space of the negative or 'nothing' – closely corresponding to that which Husserl called (and called for, but could not himself produce) a 'second *epoché*'. We will see what this space means to Shakespeare, and how it is produced in practice, in experience of the extra-theatrical, chiastic configuration of pairs of plays. Shakespeare first found his way to this second *epoché* in *Hamlet* and *As You Like It*. The indispensable first steps of this Shakespearean quest take place in *Hamlet* and in fact are exemplified by Hamlet himself.

Although *Hamlet* is often referred to as a revenge tragedy, the hero's pursuit of revenge 'with wings as swift / As meditation' (1.5.29–30) is secondary to something far more important – far more important, at least, to him. This is the disclosure to himself, precisely *in meditation*, of the inward self that he has claimed from the beginning – 'that within which passes show' (1.2.85).[1] For Hamlet-the-meditator, meditation is lived experience within language. It lives for him as self-reflection in verbal acts of theatricalisation. Yet, from the play *Hamlet* taken as a whole to *The Winter's Tale*, we see that the same breakthrough towards the disclosure of inward self reveals the necessity for escaping theatricalisation itself – and to move toward a reciprocal, intersubjective relation to an other. An escape from theatricalisation is even the condition for achieving an actuality of self and other that is finally independent of representation. Shakespeare engages in the struggle to make that exit from theatre even while repeating the chiasmus of theatricalisation as a necessary first step. That step remains imperative, in other words, for the *epoché* of consciousness in which inward self may be disclosed; and it remains vital for producing a second *epoché* that can disclose an intersubjectivity. I emphasise again that Shakespeare's efforts to overcome theatricalisation are by no means an expression of an anti-theatrical avoidance that would simply shut down, and shut out, all theatre, all representation. On the contrary, Shakespeare never wavers in seeing the necessity of working through the theatricalisation that is inherent in the human imagination and in all human experience.

Theatricalisation and Chiasmus in Hamlet

In *Hamlet* the Mousetrap is only the tip of the iceberg of theatricalisation. We are given a sense of the tight conjunction of self-reflective thinking and theatricalisation in this play in Hamlet's exhortations to the player about 'playing' in Act 3. Considering all the other matters that by that point command his attention – murder, revenge, the possible incest of his mother, usurpation of the throne of Denmark – his outbursts to the player about acting technique seem to edge toward derangement. With sustained anger, virtual rage, Hamlet shouts out that his preoccupation with *reforming* the activity of *playing* comes from the depth of his *soul*: 'O, it offends me to the soul'; 'O, there be players'; 'O, reform it altogether' (3.2.8, 27, 36). These exclamatory O, O, O's about play-acting point to something that for Hamlet is of colossal significance. When, in the same set of injunctions, he says that 'the purpose of playing . . . both at the first and now, was and is to hold as 'twere the mirror up to Nature' (3.2.20– 2) he is not merely thinking of – reflecting on – how to expose misdeeds. As we shall see, he is pointing to the mirror form and function of his own fateful deeds of theatricalisation. These acts of mirroring make possible the initiating step of Hamlet's procedure for disclosing his inward self. The three steps of that procedure are as follows: first, by acts of chiastic mirroring, momentarily suspending consciousness of the external world and of its temporality; second, discovering, in what remains to consciousness, the inward self that abides in its own temporality or special *now*; third, coming to consciousness of the external world and its temporality while retaining consciousness of his inward being in its *now*.

In Hamlet's hands the figure that repeatedly holds a mirror up to nature – always necessarily reversing what it mirrors – is, definitively, chiasmus. Hamlet conducts his primary battles not so much in physical skirmishes as in his own mental combats, which is to say with language in a world of ideas. In the great war that Hamlet wages, verbal formations frame a set of items or ideas that, as a crosswise set, blocks any complete paraphrase because it is centred in a negativity. Perhaps more intensely than any other Shakespearean hero, Hamlet faces the imagination's inherent theatricalisations. As we have noted, these are constituted by the back-and-forth movements between role-playing consciousness and a would-be non-role-playing consciousness that is, in fact, never wholly free of role-playing. Again and again, Hamlet's meditative employments – his productive thinking – of chiasmus, each endlessly moving right to left and left to right, AB:BA, ad infinitum, is his mirror held up to the theatricalised role-playing of human nature.

In Hamlet's potent negative capability, chiasmus becomes a generator of infinite progression and of experiencing the impossibility of grasping the totality of such a progression – thus producing momentary inhibitions or suspensions of consciousness of the immediate external world. T. S. Eliot famously charged that *Hamlet* is 'most certainly an artistic failure' because it fails to provide an 'objective correlative' to Hamlet's 'emotion'.[2] Partly to agree with Eliot's accusation, I note two dissonant moments in Hamlet's claims to the emotions of lover or patriot. Despite his claim to have 'loved Ophelia' more than 'forty thousand brothers' (5.1.258–60), there is little evidence (beyond Ophelia's fragmentary report of what we know to be mainly Hamlet's feigned love madness) that he has had, or has, any such emotion. Similarly, when Hamlet cries out near the end, 'This is I, Hamlet the Dane' (5.1.246) this is effectively the first we hear from him in the way of patriotic emotion. Even the interest that he apparently takes, with his very last breath, in the election of Fortinbras to the Danish throne also seems to have no 'objective correlative'. Nevertheless, Eliot's judgement here is seriously mistaken. The objective correlative to Hamlet's emotions is provided at the symbolic core of his self-revealing language. It is a correlative to emotion that is as powerfully objective as any linguistic representation can be, though (and this is what likely misled Eliot) its embodied form is enucleated, which is to say it is a negativity – a carefully framed negative capability – at the heart of all its embodied movements.

As I already suggested in Chapter 1, the particular chiasmus of theatricalisation that Hamlet offers the player hovers over all the moments of theatrical representation that, collectively, we call *Hamlet*. Challenging the player's and his own capacity to feel anything more than a theatricalised emotion – pronouncing that it is 'all for nothing' – he asks:

What's [A] Hecuba to [B] him, or [B] he to [A] her,
That he should weep for her? (2.2.492–4)

Hamlet may well sense, already, that this arch chiasmus is in fact itself 'all for nothing' of a different kind, all for a world-changing negativity. Yet it is consonant with his concealment of the sources of his suffering that he camouflages the active centrality of chiasmus in his thinking. Chiasmus comes so trippingly, so wittily, from his tongue that it hides the laborious inward struggle which produces it. We may not imagine that he is revealing anything very important about himself when, for example, he says, chiastically, 'The body is with the King, but the King is not with the body' (4.2.25–6) or 'We fat all creatures else to fat us, and we fat ourselves for maggots' (4.3.21–2). As I began to note earlier, however, Shakespeare has unmistakably signalled the importance of the figure of chiasmus in *Hamlet* by assigning Polonius an explicit statement about its *un*-importance. Speaking to Claudius and Gertrude about Hamlet's alleged madness he says, chiastically, ''tis true 'tis pity, / And pity 'tis 'tis true: a foolish figure!' (2.2.97–8). Of course there is nothing foolish about the rhetorical figure called chiasmus, except when it is used by a fool. Hamlet is no such fool. Chiasmus is his figure for approaching as nearly as possible the actuality of his inner being as well as its relation to the world. In the chiastic movements of 'The body is with the King, but the King is not with the body' Hamlet is once again driven to find a way out of the cross-purposes of theatricalisation that can doom the human condition to perpetual emptiness or inauthenticity. Hamlet's poseur addressee in this chiasmus, Claudius, represents just such emptiness. Quite likely, the power of this chiasmus is increased by an allusion to the theory of the King's two bodies (i.e. the King as both a person and an embodiment of the national community), which comes with its own intensity of role-playing.³ Certainly Hamlet here adds dangerous insult to what will be lethal injury. Intertwined with his cat-and-mouse riddle is his public announcement that within the palace of Elsinore no living body of a king, of any kind, is to be found. Among other things, Hamlet in this way insinuates that the dead body of Polonius is in the true King's domain, but the true King (Hamlet's father) has been deprived of his body – both as living man and as living embodiment of Denmark's community. In Hamlet's chiastic hands the permutations of what 'seems' and of what 'is' multiply open-endedly and dizzily.

Hamlet's chiasmata of theatricalisation frequently inform even the minutiae of his theatrical language. When, for example, he addresses the player as 'old friend' (2.2.360, 473–4) he makes an effort to step up, as it were, to the real world and to find a stable place to stand there. At the very same time, he sustains his recognition that theatricalisation always threatens to swallow the present moment. Neither the age of the player (who has only recently grown a beard) nor Hamlet's acquaintance with him is truly 'old'. Rather, the young actor is a player located in the theatrical world that exercises an irresistible attraction for Hamlet and upon which he is about to gamble with his life in the real world. Here, too, this unsettling state of affairs can be mapped as AB:BA: 'What's Hamlet (entering into play-acting) to the real-life actor called the 'old friend', or that 'old friend' to that Hamlet? A variety of the same shadow chiasmus is offered in Hamlet's whirling words about the actor who plays the King, words that, at the same time, once again point at the unwelcome man on the throne who is only an impersonator of the King: 'He that plays the King shall be welcome – his majesty shall have tribute on me' (2.2.285–6). In this contorted mirroring of violently displaced authority, Hamlet's chiasmus is itself acutely contorted. The [B] impersonal royal presence of the rightful heir to the throne (would-be non-play-acting Hamlet) shall welcome [A] the player-King: [A] the player-majesty shall have tribute from [B] Hamlet (would-be non-play-acting). Behind this chiasmus is the chiastic question, 'What's Hamlet to the player-King, or the player-King (majesty) to Hamlet?' so that we realise once again that we are never far from Hamlet's arch chiasmus of theatricalisation concerning Hecuba.

The 'Nothing' of Chiasmus: Toward the Onlooker

In Hamlet's ordeal of theatricalisation we repeatedly see him at first resisting, then embracing, the deeper implication of his own chiastic words. This is especially to be seen in his usages of 'whirling' words as a weapon against the camp of his adversaries. There, again and again, one meaning is meant to mislead his interlocutor while, at the same time, the very same words contribute to his evolving inner meditation – with its momentary bracketing of the world and his place in it. Such moments are in one sense intentional misrepresentations of a would-be surrender of being to non-being. Yet the same moments also bespeak Hamlet's struggle to effect, and to direct, an *epoché* – a 'nothing' – toward being. The latter is the meaning, for himself, that, for example, he keeps from Polonius (who has offered to take his leave from Hamlet) when Hamlet plays the suicidal melancholic, saying: 'You cannot take from me anything that I will not more willingly part withal – except my life, except my life, except my life' (2.2.210–12). Parallel to this usage, in the previous scene Ophelia misses Hamlet's doubleness (it is far more than duplicity) when she recounts his 'sigh so piteous and profound / As it did seem to ... end his being' (2.1.91–3).

Shakespeare has gone to considerable lengths to embed his authorial identification with Hamlet's ordeal of theatrical chiasmus. We have here an intimation of Shakespeare's aim to achieve for himself, down the road, an extra-theatrical *epoché* of chiastic relation and its onlooker effect. In the

Folio, Hamlet and Rosincrance (the spelling of his name in the Folio) elaborate a theatrical chiasmus that exits the play because it necessarily depends upon topical references to the London children's companies that were then damagingly competing with the established companies, including, Rosincrance informs us, the players at the Globe theatre. Hamlet asks Rosincrance, 'Do the boys carry it away?' – meaning, are the children's companies winning in this competition? – to which Rosincrance answers, in a series of near perfect chiastic reversals, '[A] Ay, that they do, [B] my lord – [B] Hercules [A] and his load too [i.e. the sign of the Globe theatre]' (2.2.358–60). The 'Ay' (confirmatory) and 'too' (replicative), as well as *they do* (*carry it away*) and *his load* (*carried away*) do more than mirror each other in reverse order. In the apposition of *my lord / Hercules* the chiasmus taps into Hamlet's earlier comparison of himself with Hercules. Claudius, Hamlet said, is 'no more like my father / Than I to Hercules' (1.2.152–3). This self-belittling comparison will be redeemed by Hamlet's heroic exertions, including, we may say, his cleansing of rotten Denmark's Augean stables. As a result, there is certainly a fitting match between 'my lord' (Hamlet) and 'Hercules'. More even than that, the behind-the-scenes – which is here to say behind-the-play – Herculean carrier of this burden of theatricalisation is Shakespeare himself, the playwright at the sign of the Globe theatre and the author of this chiasmus and of all other of Hamlet's chiasmata. I will soon have more to say about Shakespeare's ways of identifying with Hamlet's condition of theatricalisation, but Shakespeare's suggestion is here already clear that Hamlet's journey toward his *now* of inward being is, potentially at least, Shakespeare's as well. For Shakespeare these verses concerning the London theatre companies signal a breaking-out from the play to the contemporary world outside the play. Here, to be sure, Schmitt's observation concerning an *Einbruch* of contemporary anxiety about election becomes very relevant, though not in the way Schmitt imagined. Rather, a very different effect is created by the audience's, the spectator's, experience of an interminable exchange between *Einbruch* of that anxiety from the world outside the play and then an *Ausbruch* of the very same anxiety back into the contemporary world. These and further endless breakings-back-in-and-out – together create another species of *extra-theatrical* chiastic oscillation. I will shortly explain how Shakespeare channels this chiastic force, together with the extra-theatrical oscillations between *Hamlet* and *As You Like It*, to achieve the playwright's and the spectator's onlooker status.

Already here we begin to see the beginnings of the making of the condition of the Husserlian onlooker for the spectator of *Hamlet*. In this play there are two kinds of spectator of the oscillations between would-be non-play-acting versus play-acting. One kind of spectator, the sort called 'barren spectators', misses the possibility of fruitfully bracketing the world or one's life in the world. The 'necessary question of the play' that is 'then to be considered' passes over their heads (3.2.39–41). But Shakespeare makes us aware of the presence of another kind of spectator, *in potentia*, one who brings a muteness (and its affiliations with the nothing) to match Hamlet's rest that is silence. This is the living (non-play-acting) spectator in the theatre, to whom Hamlet (play-acting) turns in the gesture of linkage or handing-on that Shakespeare (from within his chiasmus of play-acting/non-play-acting) has configured. We begin to see a reflection of Hamlet's self-accusatory 'What's Hecuba to him, or he to her, / That he should weep for her?' in the chiastic address that Hamlet makes to the spectators of *Hamlet*:

[A] You that look pale [B] and tremble at this chance,
[B] That are but mutes or [A] audience to this act ...
(5.2.318–19)

In their own way these spectators are caught in theatrical cross-purposes. Their trembling is a kind of horrified speech within muteness. They look pale, as if they are on the scene of violence, yet they remain at a safe distance from the reaches of killing. These cross-purposes cannot be rationally formed into a whole idea. They function on a level of ideas and feelings that is beyond the ideas and feelings that are directly described by the infinitely progressing words of the chiasmus. On that level, we (the spectators) blink into momentary unconsciousness. In that moment we fail to take in where we are or what is happening to us. Even before entering the theatre, every spectator was already caught in his or her own condition of theatricalising imagination. Thus for each spectator now sitting in this audience, Hamlet's chiastic question booms directly over him or her as well, only in a different form: 'What's the fiction of *Hamlet* to this real life spectator, or this real life spectator to the fiction of *Hamlet* . . . that he or she should tremble, should look pale at this act?' Are we *in* this fiction? Are we *in* our lives? We, as spectators, can hope that to the extent that the spectator of Hamlet's ordeal of theatricalisation participates in it, we, too, might each reap the reward of beginning to disclose inward being in our individual *now*.

The 'Now' of Inward Being

In somewhat amplified form I wish to ask again what I take to be the primary question of this play: does Hamlet provide the grounds for his claim that he *has*, *presently* or *immediately* – in a dimension of *now* – an inward being or self that is independent of worldly experience, 'that within which passes show'? Does he already have it, and sustain it, at the moment of reproaching the Queen for not having such a thing herself (1.2.85)? Compared to this, even the question of whether 'to be or not to be' (3.1.55) is logically of secondary importance. One must first be certain one has a self, as well as the self's power of choosing, before deciding whether or not to dispose of that self. Of course it is possible to contend that there is no need to demonstrate the grounds of experience of inward being because they are self-evident. Hamlet, however, insists otherwise. He claims that the experience of such a self that he is *having* even now is what distinguishes him from the *seeming* and play-acting – the soul-deep shamming – that he sees all around him. Making his point with dagger-like sharpness, Hamlet thus declares his claim for inward being to the mother who gave him being and who, in this son's eyes, has abandoned the innermost being that she plighted to the man with whom this son was begotten:

> 'Seems', madam – nay it is, I know not 'seems' . . .
> These ['all forms, moods, shapes of grief'] indeed 'seem',
> For they are actions that a man might play,
> But I have that within which passes show,
> These are but the trappings and the suits of woe. (1.2.76–86)

Hamlet is telling Gertrude that what is left of her inner being is totally incapable of knowing *him* – this son at this moment – that she has no access to anything but his outward appearances. Later, in fact, it *seems* that he almost succeeds in getting her to 'throw away the worser part' of her being and to 'live the purer with the other half' (3.4.155–6). If she could actually manage this, it might secure her own inner *now*. But this *now* never occurs for her.

It is time to delve into the emergence of Hamlet's *now*. This *now* is the locus of suspension in which his inwardness will finally be disclosed. Nevertheless, Shakespeare will see even in Hamlet's ultimate disclosure of this important kind a failure to achieve the intersubjectivity in which alone a full human consciousness of being can be reached.

Of all the complex words in Hamlet's rich lexicon, one of the most complex, and also most evanescent, is the word 'now'. Hamlet's journey toward an ultimate location of the *now* is traced throughout the play but his arrival in that location takes place only in his last moments. Each of his usages of the *now* carries with it the shadow awareness of a demand not only for action but for consolidating the inner self that can freely choose such action. All of his thirty-two uses of the word *now* are keyed to his first, apparently perfunctory use of the word. 'What hour *now*?' he asks, when he is awaiting his first sight of the Ghost at the hour expected from Horatio's report (1.4.3; emphasis added). Hamlet's hour of the *now* is here already splitting apart. At this 'witching time' (3.2.378) a chasm opens between the world and Hamlet as well as between the spatio-temporal *now* of the spinning world and the non-spatio-temporal *now* and *presence* in which he must find his inner being. In other words, from the time of his waiting upon this hour of *now*, his life is riven between these two species of temporality, the second of which requires a sworn bonding with the whole of his innermost being.

We hear this in his very next usages of the *now*. Upon concluding his interview with the Ghost, he says, 'So, uncle, there you are. *Now to my word*. / It is 'Adieu, adieu, remember me.' / *I have sworn't*' (1.5.110–12; emphases added). He turns again from a worldly temporality to an other-worldly, indeed ghostly, *now* to make his friends swear, from their presumed innermost beings, not to reveal what they have witnessed: 'And *now*, good friends, / As you are friends, scholars, and soldiers, / Give me one poor request. . . . Never make known what you have seen tonight . . . *swear't*' (1.5.139–44; emphases added). In the middle three acts of the play Hamlet trembles, without full comprehension, on the verge of a non-worldly *now* in which he would – but cannot yet – fulfil his sworn bond, as in the following failed attempts: '*Now* I am alone. / O, what a rogue and peasant slave am I!' (2.2.484–5); "Tis *now* the very witching time of night . . . *Now* could I drink hot blood' (3.2.378–80); 'But *now* 'a is a-praying. And *now* I'll do it . . .' (3.3.73–4; emphases added). All of these *now*'s elude Hamlet because he is thus far blocked from finding his own *now* on which he might then act in the world. We could profitably explore each of his usages of *now* from this and closely related points of view but I proceed to his usages of the *now* in Act 5. Hamlet's transformed *now* finally emerges there, thus realising the potential that awaits him within his chiastic theatrical language. This transpires even in his apparently aimless drifting between poles of play-acting and would-be non-play-acting.

In the two scenes of Act 5 Hamlet marks two distinctive steps in making his way to a *now* of immediate self-presence. In the first step, reached in the graveyard scene, he fixes on the corruption of the self's *now*, the virtual degradation of the time of the self in the arrogance of mortality. The tone of these usages of the worldly *now* is set, and then sustained, from its first appearance: 'This might be the pate of a politician which this ass *now* o'erreaches – one that would circumvent God, might it not?' (73–5, emphasis added). There are seven more instances of the degraded *now* in this scene (83, 94, 96, 176, 179, 181, 182). In the second scene, and its signalling of the second step, Hamlet's perception of the *now* will finally be the effect of bracketing the world's *now* in his climactic chiasmus of theatricalisation. In this scene as a whole, a Hamlet who stands aside from – looking in on – the time of his own life, takes charge (still unilaterally) of the *now*. As if he is now suddenly capable of dispensing with the play-acting of his imagination, Hamlet tumbles into this, his final phase of being. This occurs in his excited account to Horatio of his resolute acts of survival in the sea voyage. Paradoxically, looking on at mere survival, he is *now* attaining a place to stand beyond that mere survival.

He attains to this place in the process of recounting – and perhaps already in the moments recounted. His *now* within is now becoming the lever for his self-related experience of worldly temporality. One way and/or another, his internal *now* emerges here in a storytelling *in medias res* that shifts the past time of *now* to the suspensive, dominating present of his individual *now*: 'So much for this, sir. *Now* shall you see the other' (5.2.1); 'But wilt thou hear *now* how I did proceed?' (27); '*Now* the next day / Was our sea-fight' (53); 'Does it not, think thee, stand me *now* upon?' (62) (emphases added). Hamlet's *now* now powerfully begins to open that *medias res* within the world.

The full emergence of Hamlet's inward *now* takes place as he prepares for being fully present, fully ready, for the close of his journey. This *now* is registered in phrases that are among the most cryptic and elliptical that Shakespeare ever wrote. Something is being revealed opaquely – wrenchingly – in these words, though it is unmistakable that they bind Hamlet to the present time of a threatening world. In addition, these words allow him to stand in the perpetual 'readiness' of an inward, atemporal *now*. This readiness of being is not altered by the change or becoming or forward movement of worldly time. *Now*, indeed, he can *let* the world (including his fated participation in the world) simply *be*:

> We defy augury. There is special providence in the fall of a sparrow. If it [A] be *now*, 'tis [B] not to come. If it be [B] not to come, it will [A] be *now*. If it be not *now*, yet it will come. *The readiness is all* . . . Let be. (5.2.198–202; emphases added)

Twenty lines earlier Hamlet seems to explain, in advance, this *now* of readiness, but his words there are only slightly less gnomic:

If his [the King's] fitness speaks, mine is *ready*. [A] *Now* or whensoever, [B] provided I [B] be so able as [A] *now*.
(5.2.180–1; emphases added)

Taken together these chiasmata of the explicit *now* form the endgame of Hamlet's meditative, theatrical bracketing and its products. The effect of these chiasmata is to displace all merely temporal *now*'s into the internal atemporal *now* of the readiness that cannot be touched by the world's time. This Hamlet has become an onlooker – even if still a theatrical onlooker – to his own theatrical life.

Towards the Spectator and Shakespeare as Extra-theatrical Onlookers of the Play Hamlet

For the full playing out of holding 'as 'twere the mirror up to Nature' (3.2.20–2) in this dramaturgy, Shakespeare counted on the fact that the spectator never forgets that within the play called *Hamlet* Nature is itself only a play-acting of Nature. As a result, the mirroring of Nature that fulfils the purpose of this playing is necessarily reflexive and unstoppable. In other words, *apparent non-play-acting* (what we call, or see as, 'Nature') is mirrored by *play-acting*, while, in its turn, *play-acting* mirrors back to us *apparent non-play-acting* ('Nature'), and so on forever because we only know any one of these items within the mirroring process that is endless.[4] Thus, when we experience the particular magic of theatre that *Hamlet* creates, many of us may be accessing far more than intense make-believe. If, as spectators or readers, we can inwardly experience these chiasmata for ourselves we are precipitated towards the same struggle and may begin to experience, for ourselves, the same kind of disclosure that Hamlet experiences. This is to say that we may also be gaining glimpses of recognition into our own innermost beings, in our own individual *now*. And in that *now* we may be, further, on our own way, with Shakespeare, to becoming unworldly onlookers to the performance we behold. If such is the case, we must consider the possibility that the onlooker consciousness that is thus created may at least prime us for our own experience of an intersubjectivity. More than priming, however, is necessary to produce the experience of intersubjectivity. I submit that in composing *As You Like It*, Shakespeare not only represented, theatrically, the possibilities of a new world of intersubjectivity but, more importantly, extra-theatrically realised such intersubjectivity between the playwright and spectator. He achieved this in creating a second *epoché* between *As You Like It* and *Hamlet*.

Towards Intersubjectivity

We recall that although Husserl regarded 'intersubjectivity' as the culmination of human consciousness he failed to conceptualise how it might actually, equally, be shared because he could not free himself of the idea of the one-sided dominance of the solitary or solipsistic ego.[5] Shakespeare represents and explores just such a failure to achieve intersubjectivity in Hamlet's solitary consciousness, magnificent as that consciousness certainly is even in its loneness. We may feel that Hamlet, by himself, at moments reaches toward an intersubjectivity, a sharing of consciousness. Yet Shakespeare only begins to represent a fulfilment of such consciousness in the partnership of *Hamlet* with *As You Like It*. He begins to do so by breaking past the impedances of Hamlet's lone ego into the expansiveness of Orlando's and Rosalind's reaching out to each other. From the very beginning of *As You Like It* we sense a continuity between the characterisations of Hamlet and Orlando, as well as of Hamlet and Rosalind. Although at first it may not seem to be the case, Orlando's opening outcry against 'nothing' is painfully like Hamlet's outcry of 'all for nothing'. Hamlet's 'all for nothing' appears to bemoan only the emptiness of theatricalisation while Orlando's is protesting his miserable worldly circumstances. Yet both at bottom give voice to an experience of nothingness that for them underlies life as well as its representation. And both are responding to the anxiety of the nothing in the radical displacements of brothers against brothers. Unlike Hamlet, however, Orlando will learn to make the 'nothing' of negativity the basis of his sharing, with Rosalind, in the representation (still very much theatricalised) of an intersubjectivity. These parallelisms are not either accidental or incidental. I propose that Shakespeare has made inevitable our reflection upon *Hamlet* together with *As You Like It*. Besides reinforcing our sense of both Hamlet's and Orlando's pain of the 'nothing' and their similar chiastic ways of dealing with it, this reflectiveness has a secondary effect that will turn out to be of primary significance for the impact of the two plays together.

To show, first, the parallel yet divergent ways these plays employ an *epoché* of theatricalised chiasmus, I offer parallel readings of a vivid detail that they share: namely the image of the desolate 'ungartered' lover. In *Hamlet* Ophelia reports to Polonius:

> My lord, as I was sewing in my closet
> Lord Hamlet, with his doublet all unbraced,
> No hat upon his head, his stockings fouled,
> *Ungartered* and down-gyved to his ankle,
> Pale as his shirt, his knees knocking each other,
> And with a look so piteous in purport
> As if he had been loosed out of hell
> To speak of horrors, he comes before me . . .
> He raised a sigh so piteous and profound
> As it did seem to shatter all his bulk
> And end his being. (2.1.75–93, emphasis added)[6]

In *As You Like It* Rosalind/Ganymede sets the stage for her wooing 'cure' of Orlando's love by telling him 'how a man in love' ought to appear:

> Your hose should be *ungartered*, your bonnet unbanded, your sleeve unbuttoned, your shoe untied, and everything about you demonstrating a careless desolation. But you are no such man; you are rather point-device in your accoutrements, as loving yourself than seeming the lover of any other. (3.3.316–20; emphasis added)[7]

In both of these cases we at first view the figure of the 'ungartered' lover as a transparency in which the foreground is of an apparently distraught lover while, seen behind the foreground, is an impersonation or play-acting of the distraught lover. Behind Ophelia's picturing of this lover the audience sees Hamlet's play-acting of love madness. This doubleness is symmetrical with Rosalind's accusation or worry (played out within her own impersonation) that Orlando's self-presentation as distracted Petrarchan lover is only an impersonation of the real thing. These elements of the figure of play-acting are in both cases subject to rapid exchange, so that foregrounds and backgrounds oscillate in vertiginous ways.

Rosalind does not disbelieve in Orlando's imitation-influenced love for her, though she fears that that love will prove to be short-lived.[8] When Orlando says to disguised Rosalind, 'Fair youth, I would I could make thee believe I love,' she replies from the heart of a Rosalind who wishes to get beyond play-acting by somehow using play-acting: 'Me believe it? You may as soon make her that you love believe it' (3.3.321–3). Rosalind intuits that Orlando's, as well as her own, inevitably imitative love, is in danger of slipping into mere storybook roles of lovers and beloveds. She yearns for the emergence of a love for each other that might actually, fully, be beyond play-acting. This, surely, is the challenge, and danger, faced by every lover who has ever said those endlessly quoted words, 'I love you'. Rosalind acknowledges her own lingering on the border between being 'in love' and the narcissistic, self-gratifications of playing at it – of feeding oneself with it – when she says (of other lovers), 'The sight of lovers feedeth those in love. – Bring us to this sight and you shall say I'll prove a busy actor in their play' (3.5.48–50). Certainly Rosalind is herself throughout the pre-eminent impersonator in this play. Very early on, Orlando has even intuited this element of Rosalind's own play-acting imagination. In a poem of Orlando's that Celia reads to Rosalind, Orlando has written that 'Rosalind of many parts / By heavenly synod was devised, / Of many faces, eyes, and hearts' (3.3.124–6). Between Orlando and Rosalind there is thus a suggestive mirroring of the play-acting condition, and even at least a partial consciousness of ongoing play-acting.

In *As You Like It* and *Hamlet* Shakespeare's theatrical truth-telling proceeds on the axiom that, difficult as it may be for anyone to acknowledge at first, in everyday life we are all, initially 'merely players', role-players of the identity that we wish to represent. It is indeed profoundly appropriate to the deepest aims of *As You Like It*, in its complementarity with *Hamlet*, that Shakespeare here plants the devastating metatheatrical formula, 'All the world's a stage / And all the men and women *merely players*' (2.7.139–40; emphasis added). For Shakespeare's artistic purposes in *As You Like It*, cynical Jacques is at least partially justified in making this observation about the play-acting of *most* men and women in most circumstances. In *Hamlet* the oscillations of role-playing are contemplated almost exclusively within the isolation of an individual imagination and its ego-controlled representations. In *As You Like It*, the oscillations are systematically extended to the shared, cross-purposes of play-acting between two individuals, Orlando and Rosalind. Yet these oscillations, too, remain within play-acting. The heart of *As You Like It* is Rosalind's and Orlando's search for the 'cure' of this mere role-playing within the reciprocal cross-movements of role-playing itself. This is certainly a marked advance upon the way Hamlet searches for that within himself 'which passes show' (1.1.85). Rosalind's strength derives not only from her awareness of the aspiration of the individual to overleap play-acting through *an onlooking* at play-acting; it derives, as well, from her understanding that that aspiration can only begin to be fulfilled in engagement with another individual who is doing the same thing. Rosalind's great capacity as a lover stems from her acting upon these insights and her taking in hand, necessarily with Orlando, the power of an oscillating, play-acted love that begins to produce an intersubjectivity of authentic love. That love depends upon sharing an *epoché* and its consequences in the *now* and the condition of the onlooker, and then, from the condition of the onlooker, returning to the beloved in a mutual intentionality towards life, towards being, yet in deep death-awareness.

Celia implies that in Rosalind's fall to Orlando in her *wrestling* of 'affections' she will end up on her back sexually ('a good wish upon you: you will try in time in despite of a fall' (1.3.16-18)). In fact, however, in the play as a whole the psycho-sexual implication is very strong that in leading Orlando into the cure of love she will intermittently share the lover's position of being the one on top, that is in the reciprocal passion of their play-acting imaginations. Far beyond Touchstone, she knows the truth of his observation that 'the truest poetry is the most feigning, and lovers are given to poetry; and what they swear in poetry it may be said, as lovers, they do feign' (3.4.14–16). She knows that she and Orlando must reciprocally play out the game of feigning in poetry or theatre in order to make their way toward an unfeigned love. For Hamlet and Ophelia there is not even the beginning of such possible reciprocity, so much so that Ophelia's demise takes the form of a suicidal theatre-of-one in which she plays all the parts. Hamlet does achieve a kind of overcoming of the arch play-acting that surrounds him – whether with his mother or with Rosencrantz and Guildenstern. And Hamlet does make his way to the disclosure of a self beyond play-acting. Yet, to the very end, he remains cut off from intersubjective relation, as lover, patriot or even friend. Hamlet's relation to Horatio in times of (Hamlet's own) crisis might seem to have furnished the grounds of a full intimacy of friendship. But Prince Hamlet is never equal to this egalitarian possibility. Hamlet is permanently alone, permanently exercising lone control of the representation of his world, whether outer or inner.

Wrestling

In *As You Like It* the chiastic master trope for the disclosure of the negativity of the 'nothing', as well as the movement toward a possible intersubjectivity, is the *wrestling* of self and other, other and self. Followed out and through in this wrestling, the intentionality of the 'nothing' of chiasmus is converted *toward being*. As a result of this chiastic wrestling, Orlando and Rosalind begin to share intersubjectively in a love that is again and again chiastically represented. In order to appreciate how forcefully the workings of this wrestling disclose both individual subjectivity and the beginnings of an intersubjectivity we should first note how pervasively a chiastic figure of wrestling is deployed in the fiction of *As You Like It*.

Rosalind and Orlando are continuously well matched, and are continuously sharing, in the chiastic wrestling that produces their shared nothings – the spaces of negativity opened by chiasmus:

ROSALIND: But are you [A] *so much* in love as [B] your rhymes speak?
ORLANDO: [B] Neither rhyme nor reason can express [A] *how much*. (3.3.329–30; emphases added)

ORLANDO: [A] my Rosalind [B] is virtuous.
ROSALIND: And [B] I am [A] your Rosalind. (4.1.51–2)

The meaningful 'cure' of this chiastic wrestling necessarily comes with revolutions in meaning, as in Orlando's and Rosalind's following exchange:

ORLANDO: [A] *I* would not be cured, [B] youth.
ROSALIND: [B] I would cure you if [A] you would but call me Rosalind . . . (3.3.349–51 and ff.)

In this instance the double identity that Orlando does not perceive, or perceives only unconsciously, is matched by exchanges of meaning that he does not yet comprehend, at least not consciously. Rosalind acts on a far-seeing faith. Her 'I', play-acting the 'youth' Ganymede, offers a 'cure' that would, as Orlando wishes, make his love endure. It is not a 'cure' that would, as he fears, end that love. Played out in this shared condition of having each been banished on threat of death, the chiastic game of play-acting that Rosalind proposes can, she hopes, effect the good cure, the *cura* or death-conscious *caring*, in a shared, intersubjective love.

Mirroring and Awareness of Death

As has been frequently noted, the images of wrestling and the fall of one wrestler, set out in the first scenes of *As You Like It*, proliferate in a variety of ways throughout the play in the relations of the protagonists and even in Orlando's wrestling with the lion who 'fell' at Orlando's hands. It is clear that images of wrestling have, indeed, a pivotal function in the relationship of Rosalind and Orlando. After Rosalind and Celia have looked on at Orlando's victorious wrestling match against the professional wrestler, Charles, and Celia sees that Rosalind is smitten with Orlando, Celia says to her,

'Come, come, wrestle with thy affections', to which Rosalind replies, 'O they take the part of a better wrestler than myself' (1.3.16–17). In fact, Orlando has preceded Rosalind in realising that the figure of wrestling applies to his own affections for Rosalind and that he has himself fallen within that wrestling match. In an aside he says, 'My better parts / Are all thrown down, and that which here stands up / Is but a quintain, a mere lifeless block.' Even without hearing Orlando's words, Rosalind is deep within the mutuality of this wrestling when she says to him, 'Sir, you have wrestled well and overthrown / More than your enemies.' The stage direction that immediately follows, 'They gaze upon each other', is in the play's own terms a falling for each other (1.2.201–8).

Yet the deeper significance of what occurs in falling within this chiastic wrestling is not at all obvious. What takes place there is nothing less than the reciprocal experience of an *epoché* of the nothing. This experience begins to be illuminated by noting the special effects of a double mirroring of the chiastic mirrors of self-and-other, other-and-self, such as Fink and Schütz proposed. Beyond Husserl's conceptualisations, this, we saw, was their model for achieving an intersubjectivity.[9] By registering the vital role of death-awareness in any such achievement, Schütz deepened this model, and made it even more profoundly germane to our effort to understand Shakespeare's achievement of an intersubjectivity. Schütz assigned a determinative role to the mutual directedness of an awareness of death, in both self and other. In the mirror achievement of intersubjectivity, he noted:

> of special importance is . . . that the transcendental subject must constitute itself and Others as mundane subjects . . . and that here the finitude of human being, the human fate of death, must be taken into account.[10]

If we are too much distracted by the outward festive mood of *As You Like It* we may miss the emphasis that Shakespeare has placed on the death-threat within the mirror images of wrestling (perhaps themselves mirroring Hamlet's *grappling*, serially, with the pirates [4.6.18], with Laertes in Ophelia's grave, and with Horatio to prevent him from drinking the poison). No staging of *As You Like It* can ignore the fact that at the outset three young brothers lie dying just off stage as a result of wrestling with Charles. Their 'weeping' father and the weeping gathered crowd know that there is 'little hope of life' in the fallen (1.2.100). In the same outset, Oliver compacts with Charles to make 'an end of' Orlando (1.1.128). Rosalind falls in love with Orlando at the moment when she perceives his stoic acceptance of the idea of his own death, an acceptance that he explicitly brings to his wrestling. Wrestling remains a deadly game till the end of the play when Orlando both visibly, bodily, *wrestles with himself* whether to risk his life for Oliver, who is about to be eaten by the 'hungry lioness' (4.3.121), 'Twice did he [Orlando] turn his back and purposed so' (122); and then, as noted earlier, risked his life and did indeed wrestle with the lioness, 'who quickly fell before him' (4.3.126). I propose that Shakespeare's representations of the encounter with death (of oneself or of the other), in risking the 'fall' of wrestling, entirely transforms the wrestling of play-acted love. After meeting Rosalind, Orlando begins to realise that his becoming a 'quintain, a mere lifeless block', within wrestling and fall, can *somehow* have this transformative power. We need to explain this *somehow*, just as, following Schütz's attempt to conceive of an intersubjectivity, we very much need to integrate an awareness of the human fate of death.

Orlando's opening speech, which also opens the play, underlines his being bound to 'nothing' (1.1.10, 12; cf. 24). By his statement in the next scene that he has 'nothing' in the world – 'in it I have nothing; only in the world I fill up a place, which may be better supplied when I have made it empty' –

Rosalind is moved to add her 'little strength', which is at this point, in that same world, nothing (1.2.151–3). Rosalind will incorporate this nothing or, as she will call it, this 'lack' (4.1.142), as well as her intense consciousness of the ever-present imminence of death, into the reciprocities of their play-acted wooing. When Orlando says 'For these [A] two hours, Rosalind, I will [B] leave thee,' she replies in perfect, shared chiasmus, 'dear love, I cannot [B] lack thee [A] two hours' (4.1.142–3, 148–9). The entire exchange is heightened by Shakespeare's genius for enfolding tremulous, even tragic, recognition within comic off-handedness. Thus within her role-playing hyperbole, Rosalind is actually speaking from something very like the point of death-consciousness that Orlando has assigned to the 'nothing' when she adds, in full doubleness, 'come, Death!' In this connection, Shakespeare has embedded an astonishing pun in Rosalind's decision, at her first meeting with Orlando in the forest, to 'speak to him like a saucy lackey' (3.3.250). Rosalind's wrestling with Orlando in the role of his 'saucy lackey' continually carries with it the shadow of this consciousness of mortality that is *her* thought of the 'lack', *his* of the 'nothing'. (Shakespeare returned, even more directly, to the same pun on 'lack' and 'lackey' in *Antony and Cleopatra*, 1.4.43–7.) In *As You Like It*, as in *Hamlet*, Shakespeare gives formal, not just thematic, life to this 'lack' or 'nothing'.[11] Most especially in the dynamics of chiasmus in *Hamlet* and *As You Like It*, he creates a convergence of formalism and thematics. In that convergence he creates a vast enabling of the meanings attached to negativity and to its opening of an awareness of death. The figural nothing here yields the awareness, conscious or subconscious, of the imminence of death. In its most spectacular effect this awareness can begin to bind two individuals in an intersubjectivity of consciousnesses.

To understand how such an intersubjectivity can come about in *As You Like It*, we need to see that the linkage between the 'nothing' of chiasmus and consciousness of death here depends upon another bonding element. Not surprisingly, this element has been well set out by those phenomenologists who have been intensely preoccupied with both chiasmus and intersubjectivity. That additional element is the *intentionality* to which, indeed, chiasmus is inevitably attached, whether toward being or toward non-being.

Incipiently in *Hamlet* and far more fully in *As You Like It*, Shakespeare transforms the reach of chiasmus and brings to birth, in it, the terrible beauty of an inherent consciousness of death that is centred in the 'nothing'. Although for Hamlet, too, the 'nothing' already attaches to a symbolic apprehension of death-consciousness – of 'not to be' – with him it never becomes part of a reciprocity of intentionalities. This is the case even though the figural nothingness that he achieves in his great chiasmus about the *now* in Act 5 (5.2.198–9) declares, from within chiastic language, his inescapable consciousness of the imminence of his own death. Echoing or anticipating Hamlet (depending on how we date the revisions of these plays),[12] and exceeding his ego-centred limitations, Rosalind produces a 'now' that is not only fully at home in this 'meantime' (5.4.160) or 'waste' of 'time' (2.4.88) in the forest of Arden that has 'no clock' (3.3.254); it is also deeply anchored in the necessity of reciprocal awareness.

> ROSALIND [TO ORLANDO]: Come, [A] *woo me, woo me*; [B] for *now* I am in a holiday humour and like enough to consent. [B] What would you say to me *now* [A] and I were your *very, very Rosalind*? (4.1.55–7; emphases added)

It is of the utmost importance for Shakespeare's conceiving of a possible progress toward a full human consciousness that Rosalind's and Orlando's chiasmata go beyond Hamlet's. In this wrestling with each other they achieve this by applying their emerging consciousness of death, a 'check' to 'the vital forces', to the achievement of intersubjectivity and its intentionalities. From her first employments of a chiasmus of theatricalisation, Rosalind derives its structure from the *reciprocal* wooing of wrestling. This chiasmus, this wrestling with each other, brings with it – for both wrestlers – a lover's 'fall' into the nothing and consciousness of death.

In Rosalind's and Orlando's symbolic action of chiasmus, the nothing or lack is thus not an aporetic dead-end of meaning. In their grasp of experience, which is still, however, very much bound down in representation, the fundamental structure of consciousness that creates meaning is already an intentionality; and for Rosalind and Orlando the catalyst of intentionality toward the being of the other is the immediate, all-pervading awareness of death. For both of them that awareness emerges most especially in the chiastic, reciprocal representation and rhetoric of their wrestling. The interpenetration of representational levels of this wrestling is powerfully purposive. In *As You Like It* the connection of their wrestling with awareness of death is directly evoked, for example, in Oliver's report of Orlando's being wounded in wrestling with the lion and, as a consequence, losing consciousness – and calling upon Rosalind from within that loss of consciousness: 'and now he fainted, And cried in fainting upon Rosalind' (4.3.143–4). Symmetrically, when Oliver then presents Rosalind with the napkin 'dyed in this blood' of 'the shepherd youth / That he in sport doth call his Rosalind' (151–2), Rosalind forthwith mirrors Orlando's fainting. This is a narrative thematisation of the momentary death within consciousness that is embedded in the symbolic action of their shared chiasmata – and trading places – of wrestling. There they shape their intentionality toward each other in the nothing of death-consciousness.

In *The Present Moment in Psychotherapy and Everyday Life*, the Husserlian psychoanalyst, Daniel Stern, has described the psychoanalytic interchange in chiastic terms that well fit the play of intentionality in Rosalind's and Orlando's chiasmata of theatricalisation. 'Each relational move and present moment', he says, 'is designed to express an intention relative to the inferred intentions of the other. The two end up seeking, chasing, missing, finding, and shaping each other's intentionality.'[13] Stern's account is penetrating, but in its focus on the psychotherapeutic setting it leaves out the need for sharing a deep peril – a fearfulness of death itself, for the subject as well as the other. That fearfulness is required, at the deepest level of mutual commitment, for 'shaping each other's intentionality'. This becomes the case, that is, when a full transferential responsibility for each other's very being becomes a condition of such 'seeking'. Rosalind knows that the game of chasing after each other in which she engages with Orlando is fraught with multiple perils. It is perilous not only because the world does not kindly wait upon lovers who are taking their exploratory time and not only because the outcome of the game of reciprocal play-acting can easily be a bitter, all-devouring scepticism of the possibility of any love. This game of play-acting at love is especially perilous because the consciousness of death, of the nothingness of all thought and action – the momentary loss of one's consciousness of being – attends its every motion. In the face of these deadly perils, Rosalind's faith, put to the test in the outcomes of their shared chiasmata, is that she and Orlando will live to make their way to the real thing of a sustained, shared consciousness of being. Shakespeare's tracing of their journey permits us to say that, at least as Shakespeare here represents it, the real thing of love is the shared intentionality of remaining side by side despite the omnipresent threat and the inevitability of death.

Wrestling and Intersubjectivity

That the achievement of intersubjectivity requires a two-way intentionality formed on the consciousness of death is breathtakingly affirmed in the following verses that I cited, in part, earlier:

> ORLANDO: For these [A] *two hours*, Rosalind, [B] *I will leave thee*.
> ROSALIND: Alas, dear love, [B] *I cannot lack thee* [A] *two hours*.
> ORLANDO: I must attend the Duke at dinner; by two o'clock I will be with thee again.
> ROSALIND: Aye, go your ways, go your ways. I knew what you would prove – my friends told me as much, and I thought no less. [A] *That flattering tongue of yours* [B] *won me*. [B] *'Tis but one cast away*, and [A] *so come, Death!* Two o'clock is your hour?
> ORLANDO: Aye, sweet Rosalind. (4.1.142–50; emphases added)

With her exhilarating powers of imagination and rationality Rosalind here takes Orlando along on an in inner space odyssey. There consciousness of the danger, even the inevitability, of being cast away into the nothing, into death, is what gives depth to their love. Orlando knows as well as Rosalind that there has been no time or place for the advisement of 'friends' that she fictionalises. Few moments in Shakespearean comedy are more complex than this. Here the play-acting cross-movements of Rosalind's fictionalising, in which Orlando is a silent partner, join forces with their ongoing chiastic theatricalisation. In its very delight and at its heart's core, the effect here is an intense sadness of the nothing. We are guided to seeing this effect by the knowledge that the 'flattering tongue' of Orlando that actually won Rosalind was not his Petrarchan hyperboles but his capacity for experiencing the 'nothing' that he showed in his first speaking and that he brought to wrestling with his affection for Rosalind. To his love for Rosalind, Orlando brings a continuing embrace of the 'nothing'. His early imagining of his self as 'a quintain, a mere lifeless block' is profoundly harmonious with Rosalind's later 'come, Death!' Each is reciprocally directed toward the other's continuance in being. Orlando's agreement, 'Aye, sweet Rosalind', and falling into momentary silence, richly bespeak more than he knows consciously in the reciprocities of this moment. Yet rich as they are, these are still reciprocities within play-acting. When Orlando soon says 'I can no longer live by thinking' he knows or senses, likely on more than one level, that he – they – must pass beyond their play-acting at love. Rosalind responds to Orlando's statement by exiting their charade. Taken all together, an achievement of this kind, born of chiasmus and the sublime and the momentary check to the vital forces, represents – but still only as theatricalised representation – the intersubjectivity achieved in *As You Like It* as a whole.

Besides the intersubjectivity that Rosalind and Orlando begin to achieve, at the end of *As You Like It* we discern hints of the same phenomenon in a wider access to symbolic fall. Hints toward a communal dimension of such mutual falling are seen in the proliferation of reciprocal movements of marriage celebration that confirm and extend generational bonds. Rosalind's doubled chiasmata are vividly of this kind: to her father she turns and says, 'To [A] *you* [B] *I give myself* [B] *for I am* [A] *yours*'; she then turns to Orlando with the same formula, word for word: 'To [A] *you* [B] *I give myself* [B] *for I am* [A] *yours*' (5.4.101–2). The very solemnity of this ritual of reciprocated attachment confirms the workings and effects of redoubled chiasmus with its acceptance and bestowing of a mysteriously deeper space of negativity. In this space they experience the mutual acknowledgement of a shared interval of consciousness that is outside one's control or knowledge. Similarly, Hymen diagrams communal reciprocities in a figure eight of redoubled chiasmus, of four plus four (perhaps even invoking the alchemical *chiasmos* of unity and multiplicity, the ∞) when he says, '[A] *Here's eight* that [B] must *take hands* / [B] *To join* in [A] *Hymen's bands*' (5.4.112–13). He does this while pointing suggestively to the unity within reciprocity that Rosalind and Orlando have achieved in their extended chiasmus of play-acting. Within the code of chiasmus that this play has generated, Hymen says to Orlando and Rosalind, 'You and you no cross shall part' (5.4.115). Their 'cross' or *chi*, in other words, will actually join them. Finally, Duke Senior envisions, as if in prophecy, the communal chiasmata of mutual falling in a wrestling and falling that is the dance in which Orlando and Rosalind take part at the open-ended close. Within the space of negativity in this chiasmus of *falling*, we experience a sadness that is embedded in celebration itself. The 'measure heaped in joy' is also 'heaped' in repeated, shared 'fall':

> ... [A] fall into our rustic revelry. –
> [B] play, music – and, you brides and bridegrooms all,
> [B] with measure heaped in joy [A] to th' measures fall.
> (5.4.161–2)

Towards an Extra-theatrical Intersubjectivity:
Hamlet *and* As You Like It *Together*

It is notable that the composition and/or revisions of *Hamlet* and *As You Like It* took place in the same brief period. Parts of these plays may even have been written or revised simultaneously. In fact, there are concrete indications that Shakespeare was here pursuing and even extending just such an artistry of intertwinement beyond the limits of the individual play. One cannot help noticing, for example, that, early in *As You Like It*, Adam says to Orlando, 'He that doth the ravens feed, / Yea providently caters for the sparrow, / Be comfort to my age' (2.3.43–5), while, late in *Hamlet*, Hamlet says to Horatio, 'There is a special providence in the fall of a sparrow' – just before Hamlet himself falls (5.2.197–8). So, too, Hamlet says, 'My fate cries out / And makes each petty artery in this body / As hardy as the Nemean lion's nerve' (1.4.81–3), that is, the lion that was overcome by Hercules. Orlando fulfils that fate by actually encountering and overcoming a hungry lioness (4.3.126). Even more challenging are the parallel and inversive plot relations between *Hamlet* and *As You Like It*. These relations take intertwinement to the level of unmistakable chiasmus. The order of the elements within this chiasmus follows the dominance or subordination of each item in the respective plots of these two plays. Thus:

usurping uncle Claudius		displaced niece Rosalind
is to	AS	*is to*
displaced nephew Hamlet		usurping uncle Frederick

In these interrelations Rosalind is joined by the displacement of Orlando by his brother and the banishment of Orlando by Frederick.

I propose that the fullest achievement of intersubjective consciousness in Shakespeare's composition of *Hamlet* and *As You Like It* takes place in a second-order chiastic reflection upon the chiasmata of theatricalisation that have been performed within these plays. This object of second-order reflection is the non-fictive shape made, that is, from the juxtaposed theatrical elements of both plays.[14] These elements are no longer representational, but only, purely, schematisations of representation. The chiastic object of reflection that is thus created attaches itself to, and then detaches itself from, these plays' chiastic theatricalised figures. Of these, the figure of the ungartered lover, shared by these plays, is exemplary.

Here, in paraphrase, are the disengaged elements of this formal object of reflection that, crucially, suspend theatrical suspension of disbelief itself. In other words, the chiastic working of these elements suspends belief in the fictional existence of 'Hamlet' and 'Ophelia', 'Orlando' and 'Rosalind':

> [A] 'Hamlet's play-acting of distracted lover of 'Ophelia' sets the stage for the chiastic theatricalisation of the 'Mousetrap'.
> [B] 'Rosalind's and 'Orlando's play-acting of 'Orlando' as distracted lover of 'Rosalind' sets the stage for the theatricalisation of the 'cure'?
> [B] Still very much theatricalised, 'Rosalind's and 'Orlando's movement toward a sharing of would-be-non-play-acting – in a sharing of death-consciousness of self and other – creates the theatrical representation of an intersubjectivity of *epoché*.
> [A] Still very much theatricalised, 'Hamlet's and 'Ophelia's embracings of death each reaches for an unreachable non-play-acting, thus creating a mirroring and *epoché* that could almost, but does not, constitute an intersubjectivity at a distance.

The intersubjective consciousness that Shakespeare creates from these interrelations of *Hamlet* and *As You Like It* is analogous to the sharing of an *epoché* by Rosalind and Orlando within *As You Like It*. Yet it is vastly different in being outside theatre and beyond theatricalisation. This schematised mirror reflection of chiastic actions of reduction that are themselves theatricalised mirrorings in the two plays finally escapes theatricalisation and representation. As spectators we are now in a realm where we are looking on at – experiencing from outside – not the stories represented by theatrical artifice but the formalism of the artifice itself. Mirror contemplation has now produced an extra-theatrical *epoché* and its *now* in the condition of the extra-theatrical onlooker.

The pains that Shakespeare has taken in creating this intricacy of chiastic mirrorings suggests that an intersubjective relation to his spectator or reader has all along been held out by him as an ultimate, even if deferred, goal. In the derivations of self and other, Shakespeare the onlooker finally comes to share a second *epoché* intersubjectively with the spectator-onlooker. This *epoché*, which exceeds representation, is at the centre of a replacing belief in extra-theatrical reality, a return to the world in a new condition of consciousness. Looking on from that negative space and that atemporal *now*, the playwright and spectator, standing outside the plays, share not only their coexistence but an experience of the actuality of coexistent being extended to the world around them.

Notes

1. The much debated question of whether 'a conception of personal inwardness ... existed at all in Renaissance England' is considered in detail (specifically with regard to Hamlet's claim to having 'that within which passes show') by Katharine Eisaman Maus, *Inwardness and Theater in the English Renaissance* (Chicago: University of Chicago Press, 1995), pp. 1–34, where she provides numerous contemporary attestations to its lively existence.
2. T. S. Eliot, *Selected Essays 1917–1932* (New York: Harcourt, Brace, 1932), pp. 123–4.
3. Both the chiasmus and the likely allusion to the theory of the king's two bodies have been noted here by various editors, yet the workings of the allusion within the chiasmus have seemed obscure. For the theory itself, see Ernst Kantorowicz, *The King's Two Bodies: A Study in Mediaeval Political Theology* (Princeton: Princeton University Press, 1957).
4. No doubt there is a fruitful analogy, which I will not pursue here, between Shakespeare's reflections on mirroring and Jacques Lacan's theory of the 'mirror-stage' in the development of human consciousness. Referring to Hamlet's final encounter with Laertes, Lacan, 'Desire and the Interpretation of Desire in Hamlet', ed. Jacques-Alain Miller, trans. James Hulbert, *Yale French Studies* 55/56 (1977): 11–52, wrote, 'We cannot help pausing for a moment to consider the soundness of the

connection advanced by Shakespeare, in which you will recognize the dialectic of what is already a long-familiar moment in our dialogue, the mirror stage' in which the individual engages in 'what Hegel calls the fight for pure prestige', that is, in Hegel's account of the master–slave relation (31). In the various phases of Lacan's thought he came to locate the origin of language in the loss, misrecognitions and alienations that are experienced in 'the mirror-stage', and he dismissed all forms of ego-psychology that described a distinct subject. I am suggesting that in Hamlet's language the mirror workings of chiasmus produce an unsayable gap or space of loss, yet by means of this partial annulling of language Hamlet finds a way back to the subjective self. First written in 1936, the 1949 version of 'The Mirror Stage as Formative of the Function of the I as Revealed in Psychoanalytic Experience' is included in Jacques Lacan, *Ecrits: The First Complete Edition in English*, trans. Bruce Fink (New York: Norton, 2002), pp. 75–81. Lacan continually enlarged upon the key terms of the paper. The French text was taken from transcripts of Lacan's Seminar in 1959. As Lacan's editors have recognised (*Ecrits*, p. 31) he owed his Hegelian paradigm to attendance at Alexandre Kojève's famous lectures on Hegel in Paris in the 1930s.

5. See Alfred Schütz, 'The Problem of Transcendental Intersubjectivity in Husserl (with Comments of Dorion Cairns and Eugen Fink)', trans. Fred Kersten, in *Schützian Research* 2 (2010): 16–17 and 44–5.
6. Quotations from *Hamlet* are from the Arden Shakespeare, third series, ed. Ann Thompson and Neil Taylor (London: Bloomsbury, 2006).
7. Quotations from *As You Like It* are from the New Cambridge Shakespeare, ed. Michael Hattaway (Cambridge: Cambridge University Press, 2000), from *Twelfth Night* from the New Cambridge Shakespeare edition, ed. Elizabeth Story Donno (Cambridge: Cambridge University Press, 2004). Malvolio's tormented 'cross-gartered' condition as tragi-comic would-be lover in *Twelfth Night* (2.5.127, etc.) deserves separate discussion with special attention to Shakespeare's two earlier

images of 'ungartered' lovers. It would not be surprising if the element of crossing in Malvolio's cross-gartering is found to be, on some level, a trace of the crossing between 'ungartered' role-playing lovers that Shakespeare had constructed between tragedy and comedy in *Hamlet* and *As You Like It*.

8. I am grateful to Micha Elmakies for pointing out this basic motivation, which is borne out by Rosalind's questioning of the claims of Orlando's 'rhymes'. Carmel Sharon added to this the element of Rosalind's shyness or modesty.

9. See Chapter 1 for a fuller presentation of Fink's and Schütz's model.

10. Schütz, 'The Problem of Transcendental Intersubjectivity in Husserl', 51.

11. As I noted in Chapter 1, although Paul de Man did not register the dynamics of the sublime in the workings of chiasmus, following Maurice Merleau-Ponty and other phenomenologists, in *Allegories of Reading: Figural Language in Rousseau, Nietzsche, Rilke, and Proust* (New Haven: Yale University Press, 1979), p. 49, he provided the oft-quoted formulation that 'chiasmus' comes 'into being as the result of a lack [a 'negativity'] that allows for the rotating motion of the polarities.' As I explained earlier, the precise opposite is the case. Yet there is something deeply correct in de Man's observation that the nothing or negativity within chiasmus implies a terminal *nihil*. In *The Rhetoric of Romanticism* (New York: Columbia University Press, 1984), p. 8, he argued that the 'lack' within 'chiasmic' figuration only produces a misleading 'fiction' of continued life, a masking of language's incapacity to represent meaning. In that incapacity what is called 'death', he quipped, is no more than 'a displaced name for a linguistic predicament'. Without intending to do so, de Man may well have pointed here to the productive role of death-awareness in the intentionality of chiasmus toward being.

12. I will return to the issue of the sequence of the plays shortly.

13. Daniel Stern, *The Present Moment in Psychotherapy and Everyday Life* (New York: Norton, 2004), p. 158.

14. In the *Sixth Cartesian Meditation*, p. 48, Fink describes a second-order 'phenomenology of the phenomenological reduction' as a 'making of the action of reduction the object of reflection'. As I have noted, something very like this way of proceeding from *actions of reduction* to an *object of reflection* was foreseen by Husserl as a 'second *epoché*' that he hoped would finally yield an intersubjectivity, even if a whole host of self-contradictions baffled his attempt to explain what it is or even who carries it out. On these contradictions see Schütz, 'The Problem of Transcendental Intersubjectivity in Husserl', pp. 19–25.

CHAPTER 4

THE SECOND *EPOCHÉ* OF *OTHELLO* AND *THE MERCHANT OF VENICE*

In the partnership of *The Merchant of Venice* and *Othello* the *epochés* that are produced within the chiasmata of theatricalisation of each play are transformed by an over-chiasmus between the plays that is a conceptual object of reflection. Contemplating – onlooking – that chiastic object, which is outside theatre, opens a second *epoché*. For the playwright and spectator as onlookers to that object, the second *epoché* makes possible the condition of intersubjective consciousness. In that condition, consciousness is experienced in a reciprocity of intentionality between self and other.

The Merchant of Venice and *Othello* are twinned so extensively that it is tempting to believe that, already in composing *The Merchant of Venice*, Shakespeare prepared for the possibility, even the necessity, of providing a mirroring between this play and a future other play. Yet whatever that case may have been, what is certain is that by the time he completed the composition of *Hamlet* and *As You Like It* he saw clearly how such a twinning of plays could be fulfilled and what it might produce. In pursuit of such a fulfilment between *Othello* and *The Merchant of Venice*, the figure of chiasmus, and even of an over-chiasmus, again became central to his design. Although the full range of this design remains far beyond Othello's experience or understanding, he himself schematises its essential structure when in his final speech he says that he was 'Perplexed in the extreme' (5.2.342). 'Perplexed' indeed. No matter how much we intensify the meaning of bewilderment carried by the word, in this play it continues to cry out for probing its covered-over recesses of agony and catastrophe. These are made partly accessible by noting the rich Latin and Greek etymology of the word *perplexed* – *plectere, plexus, πλόκ-ανον, πλεκ-τή* – which includes, indeed, a network or net of meanings such as those of a *web, something braided* or *woven, entangling, ambiguous*, a *web of deceit*, even a *forming of the plot* of a tragedy. The 'in the extreme' in which Othello has been entangled is a braiding of particular polarities or extremes. Othello tells a frightened Desdemona that there is 'magic in the web' of the handkerchief that she has lost: 'To lose't or give't away were such perdition / As *nothing* else could match' (3.4.62–5; emphasis added). We will see that, throughout *Othello*, chiasmata and their nothings constitute a magic of the entangling web in which Othello's – and Desdemona's – perdition will be matched, or demonically made, from a nothing. In ever expanding complexity, the magic of that web will finally become part of a different kind of web or braiding beyond the play.

Even at the level of plot, *The Merchant of Venice* and *Othello* are partnered far more extensively and intricately than being plays about Venice and deep prejudice. Certainly in these prima facie regards, the two plays already mirror each other point for point. Together they form a chiasm from the chiastic tensions between self and other, other and self, within each play. Both plays, that is, have the spectacle of bolted daughters at their cores. In *The Merchant of Venice*, the daughter of the detested race (the Jew, forever *other*) is coupled with a white Christian (the *self* that is identified with the audience) in mirror opposition to the Antonio (the *self* that is identified with the audience) threatened by the Jew (the *other*). In *Othello* – precisely in mirror reversal – the daughter of the white Christian (the *self* that is identified with the audience) is coupled with the man of the detested race, the black other, in mirror opposition to black Othello (the *other*) threatened by white Iago (the disturbing incarnation of the audience's racist *self*).

If there were any doubt about Shakespeare's intentional coupling or mirroring of these couplings in this way, it is dispelled by the way Iago provides (for the spectator or reader) an echo chamber of the shared plight of the fathers of these two daughters. After Jessica has fled in the night and handed her father's treasure to Lorenzo and his band of high-spirited 'thieves' (2.6.23), Shylock's shouting is quoted with relish by Solanio: 'My ducats and my daughter! A sealed bag, two sealed bags of ducats' (2.8.17–18). Just so, Iago energetically vexes the father of the other daughter to the same nightmare: 'Awake! What ho, Brabantio! Thieves, thieves! Look to your house, your daughter, and your bags! Thieves, thieves!' (1.1.80–2). Of course, Iago has no access to the extra-theatrical point of view that Shakespeare opens for the spectator of the two plays together.

Thus, too, as part of the manifest signs of continuity between these plays, the Gratiano who suddenly appears at the end of *Othello*, and who is designated as the inheritor of Othello's worldly substance, is a transmutation of the Gratiano of *The Merchant of Venice*. It may even be that the last words of the Gratiano of *Othello*, 'All that's *spoke* is marred!' (5.2.353; emphasis added), bear two very different meanings: one, directed to the protagonists of this play, records Othello's spoiling of his eloquent speech by his bloody suicide; the other, exiting the play proper, is spoken to Gratiano's earlier incarnation in *The Merchant of Venice*, the man who 'speaks an infinite deal' of worldly 'nothing'. The Gratiano of *Othello* points suggestively to an unworldly nothingness of silence that *speaking* can only mar.

In fact, one of the deepest continuities between *The Merchant of Venice* and *Othello* is created by the grim afterlife of Gratiano's joke on Nerissa's vaginal 'no other thing' – the joke with which the earlier play signs off. The nihilistic nothing that is repeatedly represented in *Othello* is an extreme instance of a male insatiability, an always incomplete, imagined half-knowledge of the female sexual space. The whole run of Iago's dehumanised nothings is a serial injection of the venom of his 'Nothing, my lord; or if – I know not what' deeper and deeper into Othello's brain. Here I wish to amplify my comments on this 'nothing' in Chapter 1.

Iago inserts this chiasmus and its *epoché* of nothing into Othello's imagination during the following exchange after their viewing of the (innocent) meeting between Desdemona and Cassio that Iago has engineered:

> IAGO: Ha, I like not *that*.
> OTHELLO: What dost thou say?
> IAGO: *Nothing, my lord; or if – I know not what.*
> OTHELLO: Was not that Cassio parted from my wife?
> IAGO: Cassio, my lord? No, sure, I cannot think it
> That he would steal away so guilty-like,
> Seeing your coming.
> OTHELLO: I do believe 'twas he. (3.3.35–9; emphases added)

Iago converts the simple deictic 'that' into the unknowable 'what' of the entangling 'nothing'. Yet the nothing that Iago actually names is far less deadly than the invasive nothing that is produced within the inaudible, invisible effect of his chiastic language:

> [A] Nothing, my lord;
> [B] or if –
> [B] I know not
> [A] what.

Iago has already told us, chiastically, a good deal about his own inhuman relation to that 'what':

[A] I am
[B] not
[B] what [*a* quid *or thing that is not the thing*]
[A] I am. (1.1.66)

Iago's demonic power over Othello derives chiastically both from the illimitable nothingness of Iago's dehumanised 'what' and from his bringing to bear, again and again, the disruptive force of the sexualised 'nothing'. More than anything else, these are the power and the force of the nothing that will leverage Othello out of existence.

Othello's immediate receptivity to Iago's manipulation of this nothing suggests how strongly the space of the negative already bears this sexual potentiality for his imagination. Othello's imagination is a fertile soil for such agonised envisaging. When, in response to Desdemona's suit on behalf of Cassio, Othello says

Prithee no more. *Let him come when he will*;
I will deny thee nothing (3.3.75–6; emphasis added)

and then repeats, 'I will deny thee nothing' (83), a part of Othello's mind, perhaps only in its unconscious depths, is playing pimp to her imagined whoredom of the 'nothing' with a libidinous Cassio: 'Let him come when he will'. (In the same year as the first recorded performance of *Othello*, Thomas Dekker and Thomas Middleton heavily employed the language of 'come' as sexual orgasm in Part One of *The Honest Whore* [London, 1604], 1.2.1–5.) This is to say that Iago's twisted language thus matches an accessibility in the twistedness of Othello's imagination that pushes the spectator or reader to readings that may at first seem bizarre.

Another example of this phenomenon transpires in the following verses, where Othello's elaborately imagined 'So I had *nothing* known' not only expresses aversion, but also hints, in entangled perplexity, at a voyeuristic desire for vicarious experience of Desdemona's would-be promiscuous doings in the space of her nothing:

> OTHELLO: I had been happy if the general camp,
> Pioners and all, had tasted her sweet body,
> *So I had nothing known.* (3.3.346–8; emphases added)

This 'nothing', in other unspoken words, makes its own tormenting sense, in its own grammar, in this case meaning – or rather, unconsciously gesturing toward meaning – '*so / thus (in this vicarious way) I had known the nothing*'. Similar effects are wrought in a long series of nothings, whether imposed by Iago or all too easily taken on by Othello:

> IAGO: Nay, yet be wise; yet *we see nothing done* [meaning, *we picture, we cannot help endlessly imagining, the doings in that nothing*] . . . (3.3.433; emphases added)

> OTHELLO: *For nothing canst thou to damnation add* [meaning, or rather, tumbling into, *you can add the sexual nothing to damnation*]
> Greater than that. (3.3.373–4; emphases added)

> IAGO: Would you, the supervisor, grossly gape on?
> Behold her topped?
> OTHELLO: *Death and damnation! O!* [*this is the O of the nothing and of O̲thello's helpless attraction to imagining its doings*] (3.3.395–6; emphases added)

> OTHELLO TO DESDEMONA (about the missing handkerchief) – seen earlier:
> To lose or give't away were such perdition

> *As nothing else could match.* [*meaning that giving away the handkerchief matches the adulterous fornication in her space of the nothing*] (3.4.63–4; emphases added)

Iago understands the workings, in Othello's imagination, of just this equation of *doing the nothing with 'any man'* and *giving away Othello's handkerchief*:

> IAGO: Will you think so?
> OTHELLO: Think so, Iago?
> IAGO: What,
> To kiss in private?
> OTHELLO: An unauthorized kiss!
> IAGO: Or to be naked with her friend in bed
> An hour or more, not meaning any harm?
> OTHELLO: Naked in bed, Iago, and not mean harm?
> It is hypocrisy against the devil.
> They that mean virtuously, and yet do so,
> The devil their virtue tempts, and they tempt heaven.
> IAGO: *So they do nothing*, 'tis a venial [excusable] slip.
> But if I give my wife a handkerchief –
> OTHELLO: What then?
> IAGO: Why then 'tis hers, my lord; and being hers,
> She may, I think, bestow't [the maddening *it!*] on *any man*.
> (4.1.1–13; emphases added)

> IAGO: Or I shall say you're all in all in spleen
> And *nothing of a man*. [*hinting at Othello's being impotently displaced in access to Desdemona's nothing?*]
> (4.1.86–7; emphases added)

From the time that Iago begins to plague him, Othello's mind is wrapped in thick mists, so that we cannot be sure that we understand his responses to any one of these nothings. It is certain, however, that, poisoned by Iago's nothings, Othello (like Leontes in *The Winter's Tale*) drives himself to the annihilation of his personality. He becomes 'nothing of a man' because he cannot control his imagination of the sexually rampant nothing, which, he agonisingly imagines, hides under his wife's 'mask':

> OTHELLO TO EMILIA: You have seen *nothing*, then? . . .
> Nor send you out o'th'way? . . .
> To fetch her fan, her gloves, her mask, nor *nothing*? (4.2.1–9; emphases added)

The Epoché *of the Nothing in* Othello

All the means of producing an *epoché* of the nothing that we encountered in *The Merchant of Venice* are replicated in *Othello*. These are, in sum:

1. the deployment of an effectively open-ended series of the 'nothing';
2. a series of the protagonists' chiasmata, with their *epochés*;
3. a suspension of belief in the protagonists' theatricalisations;
4. a chiasmus of the *Einbruch* and *Ausbruch*, and *Ausbruch* and *Einbruch*, of the racism of Shakespeare's contemporary English audience.

Othello's and Desdemona's chiasmata, with their *epochés* of the nothing, move toward a death-awareness of self and other. If reciprocally realised toward each other, these might have created an intersubjectivity worthy of the name of love. Yet for Othello death-awareness remains limited to fear of his self's 'Perdition' under the threat, as he sees it, of Desdemona's perfidious, annihilating being:

> [A] Perdition catch my soul
> [B] But I do love thee [= *if I love thee not*];
> [B] And when I love thee not,
> [A] Chaos is come again. (3.3.90–2)

Othello's 'nothing' of hatred, intended indeed to bring about Desdemona's non-being or death, horrifyingly resembles Iago's toward Othello:

OTHELLO:
[A] Yield up, O love, [*already the tyrannical command of hate*]
[B] thy crown
[B] and hearted throne
[A] To tyrannous hate! (3.3.449–50)

Only in Desdemona's and Othello's very last instants of life does Shakespeare allow each of them a reaching out toward the other in a full recognition of the mortality of self and other, that is, in a fully reciprocal intentionality toward the sustaining of – or yearning for – each other's being, each other's life, at – or past – the gates of death:

DESDEMONA:
[A] Farewell.
[B] Commend me to my lord.
[B] O [*her final commendation; and with the initial of her lord*]
[A] farewell! (5.2.125–6)

OTHELLO (in the first quarto):
[A] O
[B] *Desdemona,*
[B] *Desdemona,* dead,
[A] O, o, o (5.2.279)

OTHELLO:
[A] I kissed thee ere I killed thee:
[B] no way but this [*i.e. killing myself*],
[B] Killing myself,
[A] to die upon a kiss. (5.2.354–5)

It is notable that, whether directed toward non-being or, too late, directed toward being, each of these chiasmata continues to be limited to a one-sided ego-dominance of theatricalisation – a residual illusion of lone representational control of actuality. The effect of the progression of the chiasmata and their nothings throughout the play moves them toward an extra-theatrical *epoché* that escapes this illusion. Yet the full realisation of that extra-theatrical *epoché* will have to be won by other means.

Suspension of Belief in the Protagonists' Theatricalisations

Within *Othello*, Shakespeare's measures against theatricalisation are more radical than in *The Merchant of Venice*. In *Othello* they amount to the pitching of theatricalisations broadside against each other, with the effect of suspending belief not only in the felt emotion of hatred claimed by protagonist-Iago but even – inconceivable as this may at first seem – suspending belief in the love repeatedly claimed by protagonist-Othello and protagonist-Desdemona. It has often been noted that Shakespeare has cast Iago as a kind of playwright, thus, by analogy, seeming to put his own artistic credibility, or integrity, in question. I suggest that Shakespeare's aim in this matter is something else. His move beyond theatricalisation – his breaking the fiction of the play itself – begins to emerge in the *epoché* of deep doubt or disbelief created, in tandem and chiastically, by both sides of the play's theatricalising protagonists. Not only Iago, but Othello and Desdemona as well, are cast in the roles of scripting their own theatricalisations, their own manufacture of avowed feelings and their effects. Iago scripts his way to knavery as he goes along:

> Cassio's a proper man: let me see now;
> To get his place and to plume up my will

> In double knavery. How, how? Let's see:
> After some time, to abuse Othello's ear
> That he is too familiar with his wife;
> He hath a person and a smooth dispose
> To be suspected, framed to make women false.
> The Moor is of a free and open nature,
> That thinks men honest that but seem to be so,
> And will as tenderly be led by the nose
> As asses are.
> I have't. It is engender'd. Hell and night
> Must bring this monstrous birth to the world's light.
> (1.3.374–86)

Iago's alleged discovery of Hell's potency within him, like his later 'Diabolo, ho!' (2.3.142), 'Divinity of hell!' (2.3.317), only confirm his own hellish total imprisonment in theatricalisation. Within that theatricalisation the emergence of a nothing, aimed only at non-being, is an inevitability. His last words, 'Demand me *nothing*; what you know you know. / From this time forth I never will speak word' (5.2.300–1; emphasis added) are mouthed by someone who has been written out of existence by his own emptiness of theatricalisation. The elliptical construction of 'Demand me nothing' hints that the *nothing* has now demanded, commanded, Iago's dissolution. We hear no more of Iago because he has been completely swallowed up by the nothing, toward non-being, of that theatricalisation.

It may go against our instinctive sympathy with Othello's and Desdemona's terrible suffering but I propose that Shakespeare has put their vaunted love in almost as deep doubt as Iago's claims to passionate, personal hatred. Belief in their alleged love is finally suspended by the spectator to close to the same degree as in Iago's averred hate. In fact, promoting this near symmetry, their theatricalised love is juxtaposed with Iago's theatricalised hate in the same early scene. Here is Othello's account of the 'process' of writing his script and how Desdemona helped block it out:

> It was my hint [opportunity] to speak – such was the process:
> . . . This to hear
> Would Desdemona seriously incline;
> But still the house affairs would draw her thence,
> Which ever as she could with haste dispatch
> She'd come again, and with a greedy ear
> Devour up my discourse; which I observing
> Took once a pliant hour and found good means
> To draw from her a prayer of earnest heart
> That I would all my pilgrimage dilate
> Whereof by parcels she had something heard,
> But not intentively. I did consent,
> And often did beguile her of her tears
> When I did speak of some distressful stroke
> That my youth suffered. My story being done,
> She gave me for my pains a world of sighs;
> She swore, in faith, 'twas strange, 'twas passing strange,
> 'Twas pitiful, 'twas wondrous pitiful;
> She wished she had not heard it, yet she wished
> That heaven had made her such a man. She thanked me,
> And bade me, if I had a friend that loved her,
> I should but teach him how to tell my story,
> And that would woo her. Upon this hint I spake:
> She loved me for the dangers I had passed,
> And I loved her that she did pity them. (1.3.141–67)

Following this 'process' step by deliberate step reveals to us that what Desdemona and Othello 'loved', respectively, was Othello's self-dramatisation and Desdemona's keen receptivity to such self-dramatisation. Many or most of us will be hard put to believe that this is the love of one human being for the present reality of another human being, not for his theatrical 'story' or for her 'sighs' at his skilful theatrical telling. Even before we acquire Shakespeare's vocabulary for the experience of the nothing of theatricalisation, it is impossible not to sense that Othello's and Desdemona's deep immersion in the effects of self-dramatisation – of theatricalisation – will inevitably lead to something very like a nothing of non-being. Yet the spectator to this play and its partner play, *The Merchant of Venice*, is propelled by the same structures of theatricalisation toward a realm beyond theatricalisation and to a nothing in an intentionality toward being.

Mirrored Einbruch / Ausbruch, // Ausbruch / Einbruch *between the Two Plays*

The lurch – the *epoché* – in which these theatricalisations leave us in *Othello* is reinforced by an expedient that closely duplicates the breaking of theatrical illusion in *The Merchant of Venice*. In the earlier play, we saw, this is accomplished (among other ways) when the English audience of this Venetian tale is reminded of its special taste for English trial by jury. This takes place in Gratiano's joke about the twelve so-called 'godfathers' who send a condemned man to the noose of the 'gallows' and to God's judgement (4.1.393–6). In *Othello*, speaking of the drinking song with which he is ensnaring Cassio, Iago snaps theatrical illusion by directly addressing the English audience and even making them – from outside the play – an extra-theatrical, third party to the on-stage villainy of the 'nothing' that he aims at Othello:

> I learned it in England, where indeed they are most potent in potting. Your Dane, your German, and your swag-bellied Hollander – drink, ho! – are *nothing* to your English ... O sweet England! (2.3.66–75; emphasis added)

As in the case of *The Merchant of Venice*, *Othello* plays upon, plays with, the all-too-human weaknesses of its English audience, in this case a harmless proclivity to beer-drinking. But the very harmlessness of this 'English' fault serves as a sinister cover for the toxic failing that is the central preoccupation of this play: namely this audience's (many audiences', but at this particular moment, this audience's) entrenched racial prejudice against the black other. In this play, too, therefore an inevitable part of this audience's experience of the play is the chiastic effect of an oscillation between *Einbruch* and *Ausbruch*, *Ausbruch* and *Einbruch* of the contemporary historicity of this racism. In other words, at every moment of this theatrical production the members of this audience are catapulted into and out of their real and represented racism towards blacks – perhaps less than the racism towards Jews, but not much less. In turning from the play to his English audience, Iago knows exactly how to weave 'sweet England' into his chiastic web and its abyss of a dehumanised 'nothing'. In *Othello*, as in *The Merchant of Venice*, the oscillations of *Einbruch* and *Ausbruch* smoothly join forces with the protagonists' chiastic theatricalisations. Here, too, the totality of these forces open an experience that is beyond the reach of anyone within the play. This experience only becomes available to the playwright and the spectator in their condition as onlookers.

In reading *The Merchant of Venice* I tried to demonstrate the relevance of Husserl's proposition that the experience of an 'un-humanisation', a bracketing of a prejudgemental humanness in the *epoché*, leaves the mind open to the disclosure of an unprejudiced grasp of the human. I suggested that in *The Merchant of Venice* the disclosure of such an *epoché* is projected beyond the play by the instrumentality of the play. Husserl was confident – at least throughout most of his career (before the rise of Hitler) – that such an 'un-humanisation' was in no danger of collapsing into a dehumanisation. In something like the same measure, he was confident that a true intersubjectivity of consciousness would somehow be the end result of the work of bracketing that produces the *epoché*. Shakespeare continually saw lurking a darker side of the *epoché* and a deep danger in any un-humanisation. We are meant to be disturbed by Shakespeare's ending *The Merchant of Venice* with Gratiano's pudendal joke just after a life and death contest has been enacted. That play's heady, festive conclusion is intentionally left facile, suspended toward a remediation and completion elsewhere. Clearly, no intersubjectivity of consciousness is achieved there between the antagonists within that fiction. Yet for Shakespeare this is not the end of the story, or rather there is another, non-fictive enactment that is now to be experienced. This is an enactment of poetic intention – of achieved intentionality. All told, but subtractively beyond any storytelling, this will yield a very different drama of consciousness. Now, half a dozen years after writing *The Merchant of Venice*, Shakespeare brings to fruition – in the pairing with *Othello* – the potentiality of a second *epoché* that he has learned from writing *Hamlet* and *As You Like It*.

Conversion and Second Epoché *from the Chiastic Object of Reflection between the Plays*

I propose that the web of chiastic language in *Othello* achieves, together with *The Merchant of Venice*, the web of a second *epoché* that veers away from the plays' dehumanisations toward a suspensive un-humanisation that is experienced by the playwright and spectator. The same second *epoché* makes possible the beginnings of an actual intersubjectivity. Shakespeare recognises that the achievements of an *epoché* in the chiasmata of theatricalisation are not sufficient for achieving the goals of either a suspensive un-humanisation or an intersubjectivity. This is the case because the theatricalising ego (even, by identification, the playwright's or spectator's ego) wields the *epoché* to bolster its own being at the expense of the being of the effaced other. A total severing of the self's dominance over the *epoché* becomes a bare necessity if any equality and reciprocity of self and other can begin to be imagined. As in the case of *The Merchant of Venice*, in *Othello* this severing is achieved not within but through the instrumentality of the play – ultimately, once again, between the two plays seen from outside both plays by the playwright and the spectator as onlookers.

To begin to sum up and to qualify what we have seen: From these plays a second *epoché* is produced through the formation of a chiastic object of reflection. This takes place in the mirroring of chiasmata (which are themselves mirrors) within each play that are yet anchored in the illusions of theatricalisation and representation. As in the case of *Hamlet* and *As You Like It*, contemplating *Othello* and *The Merchant of Venice* together, extra-theatrically, in conceptual, chiastic form, produces an object of reflection that is outside theatricalisation. Braided into a single object of reflection, each of its elements has been extracted from its fiction or suspension of disbelief. As a result, the chiastic mirroring of actions of chiastic mirroring that have taken place in both plays *now* discloses a replacing belief in extra-theatrical reality. This belief – experience lived in this belief – marks a return to the world in a new condition of consciousness. Looking on from a shared negative space and an atemporal *now*, the playwright and spectator, outside the plays, share not only the coexistence of their own beings but – as in the joint experience of *Hamlet* and *As You Like It* – an experience of actuality in its extended extra-theatrical being.

Yet, as I suggested earlier, Shakespeare does not express unqualified confidence in an assured human outcome after the phase of suspensive un-humanisation has been achieved. The twinning of these Venetian plays and their theatricalisations of intractable racism (of self versus other and back, endlessly) can indeed produce a more total *epoché* and an enabling un-humanisation. Thus, too, the symmetries that we have described, even the obvious asymmetries (that we have not described) between the mythical or folkloric origins of anti-Semitism and racism, can take their place within the chiasm of sameness and difference that joins these two plays. And, further, the great object of reflection that is thus produced stands beyond the reach of any self-interested representation of the human. As a result, reflecting on it can – might – indeed serve as a halfway house toward a rehabilitation, even a revelation, of the human. Yet the last leg of this journey must take place in a territory for which Shakespeare offers no chart, only a vehicle of transportation, of transformation. He addresses and joins us – as spectators, as readers – on our way *toward* the human in a shared consciousness of disinterested human subjectivities. In this intersubjective condition we *can* find, we *can* make, the human – as it were, on the road. To paraphrase and to look ahead to Kent at the end of *King Lear*, this is the 'journey . . . shortly to go' to which the unseen other presently 'calls me'. This is the offer of a journey for which 'no' must not be the response, even if, ironically, the transit is wholly through a negativity. As Kent saw from the beginning, this is a journey toward being in the Cordelian 'nothing'.

CHAPTER 5

INTENTIONALITY TOWARD BEING: BLESSING IN *KING LEAR* AND *THE WINTER'S TALE*

In *King Lear* and *The Winter's Tale* Shakespeare once again anticipates and goes beyond Husserl's ways of disclosing actuality. Shakespeare does this by showing how the intentionality that is required for knowing that actuality must and can be achieved in an intersubjectivity. Shakespeare shows how intersubjectivity is in practice built on the sharing of an awareness of mortality and on the intention of a 'benediction' (the key to Cordelia's being) for sustained being of the other. Here, too, here prodigiously, in the reflection on the two plays together the 'nothing' of a double *epoché* enables the full realisation of such intersubjective, intentional consciousness. This fulfilment takes place, beyond all theatricalisation, for the onlooker playwright and the onlooker spectator.

Nothing and Blessing in King Lear

The most telling fact about the design of *King Lear* is that it concludes with a fulfilment of the action that first sets the tragedy in motion, namely the division – more accurately the distribution – of the kingdom. It may be objected that it is not this action but rather Lear's so-called love test that catapults the protagonists into tragedy. The love test, however, is only an expression of a larger impulse that this play continually represents, namely the drive towards achieving shared consciousness of being itself. Implicit in this aim is the idea, shared by many thinkers and writers, that we only have experience of the being of our ego or self when it is engaged in a reciprocity of recognition with an other. For Shakespeare this idea finds its defining expression in a reciprocal intentionality of blessing – aimed, in other words, at maintaining the being of each other. As we have seen, Shakespeare's version of this idea repeatedly finds its practical attainment to suspension and deferral of self in the condition of the 'nothing' or *epoché*. As we have also observed, Shakespeare ultimately aims at an *epoché* or nothing that exceeds the chiasmata of theatricalisation that initially produce it. And, as a result, a unique experience and a unique knowledge will be made available, although only to be shared fully by the playwright and the spectator. Yet even within *King Lear* there are gigantic pointers to that experience and knowledge. Cordelia's 'nothing' comprehends and cryptically represents this knowledge from the beginning. So, too, even though Lear's scheme of sharing in worldly being produces deception and selfishness, he, also, will later show that his core longing is for a shared consciousness of inner being that is centred in attainment to Cordelia's species of the 'nothing'. All too briefly he will achieve this goal in reciprocal, chiastic blessing of the nothing with Cordelia – as will Gloucester (also all too briefly) with Edgar. These tragic moments of aborted blessing crown the communal drama of *King Lear*. Indeed, it is definitive of the workings of this play that the partial fulfilments that these exemplary moments represent are achieved collectively through transformative interactions of language and consciousness among Lear, Cordelia, Gloucester and Edgar, as well as the Fool, Kent and Albany.

These collective transformations are wrought in many ways, most visibly by effectively endless repetition of the narrative unit – the compact rehearsal of eradication – that links the protagonists' suffering, especially their acute humiliation. Humiliation of this order is the impact on the ego of giant affliction – the effect of being humbled without limit, crushed and mortified *in extremis*. A narrative of such endlessly repeated humiliation finally works against narrative in that it tends to obliterate the time and place coordinates of narrative. In this narrative process, at the points of virtual annihilation – of reduction to *nihil*, nothing – the possibilities of transformation unexpectedly open wide. I will refer to this repetition of humiliations as the zero narrative because of its negating effects but also because Shakespeare here painstakingly coordinates it with the transformative language of the 'nothing'. Together the collective zero narrative and the language of the 'nothing' enable the emergence of a reciprocally aimed consciousness of being.[1] Kenneth Burke famously suggested that literature can provide indispensable 'equipment for living'.[2] Indeed, in *King Lear* Shakespeare brings to bear the colossal impact of a collective zero narrative and a language of the 'nothing' in order to disclose, together, an intense and immediate consciousness of being itself.[3] *King Lear* suggests why at any moment, at any age, humanity is defined by its potentiality for the rebirth of such consciousness. In its overwhelming power of bringing us to the verge of this rebirth, *King Lear* has no rivals in Western literature, except perhaps for Sophocles's *Oedipus at Colonus*, to which, we will see, *King Lear* is intimately related. Yet we must be clear about who finally gains access to this equipment for living in Shakespeare's (or in Sophocles's) dramatic art. At the furthest reach of that theatrical – in fact, that post-theatricalising – art, this equipment for living becomes jointly available only to the consciousnesses of the playwright and the spectator. For that reason, it will be important to remind ourselves continually that what transpires within these plays is for Shakespeare, even at its most intense, preliminary to something else. I return now, however, to the invaluable pointers towards this equipment that *King Lear* itself provides.

The Zero Narrative

One reason that *King Lear* forces us to seek for a collective narrative is that its victim-protagonists are continually crushed together. Parallels and mirrorings of scenes of misfortune make this pressure of agglomeration clear throughout the play. This effect is represented paradigmatically in the collective suffering of the storm scene but it is continually felt in the inexorable piling up of tragic consequences. A second reason that we attend to these characters as a group who play out a single bedrock story is the way they trade places across lines of social caste. This interknitting does not make them a herd, but rather a variegated community of free-willed individuals. Thus a nameless, formerly loyal serving man steps forth as the challenger to his ducal master, the Fool mordantly disciplines the King, Kent becomes a servant who keeps his own spontaneous counsel, while Edgar metamorphoses into a 'beggarman' (4.1.29) whose resourcefulness, as a beggar, sustains an outcast earl.[4] In their shared story of affliction these and other protagonists huddle under the arc of a common humanity. We do not need to sign on to any one humanist essentialism in order to recognise that the driven rout of this tragedy does not struggle simply to stay alive. Rather, they agonise to achieve, in consort, an irreducible expression of the human – irreducible, to them at least, as 'unaccommodated' (3.4.95–6) women and men.

In the world of *King Lear* individuals grope toward shared being in terrifying aloneness, but they begin to attain it by completing a circuit of humiliations with other individuals. The activity and meaning of this circuit are not immediately apparent. In order to comprehend it we are forced to learn a new language that the protagonists of this tragedy speak collectively, which is to say most often even without individual awareness of the collective meanings of that language.

Gloucester describes Edgar as one 'whom the heavens' plagues / Have humbled to all strokes' (4.1.59–60). *Mutatis mutandis*, the same description applies to Gloucester himself and to Lear, Cordelia, the Fool and Kent. *King Lear* is a spectacle of high-speed, relentless humiliations. The Fool warns Kent, who has hitched his fate to Lear's, 'let go thy hold when a great wheel runs down a hill' (2.4.65–6) – as if this wheel is itself a monstrous cipher that swallows all those who are around Lear. Lear adopts the Fool's metaphor of the careening wheel and gives it an even more destructive, more energetic signification: 'I am bound / Upon a wheel of fire' (4.6.43–4). This intensification of the metaphor of the wheel corresponds to Lear's experience of an energy of destruction that is raised to ever higher powers. In like manner, Edgar's imagined 'worst' case of humbling strokes is forced down to ever more total erasure. Beyond becoming fugitive and beggared, he must yet witness not only his father's blinded, bleeding eyes, his father's loss of any desire to live, but also, when comfort seems at hand, the bursting of his father's heart, a calamity for which Edgar will blame himself. And in all this, Edgar has not yet reached the climax of his afflictions. 'The worst is not,' he realises, 'So long as we can say "This is the worst"' (4.1.28–9). According to the logic of tragic process that issues from this realisation, (1) imagining the true worst case is only possible in a stage *after* an unrelenting series of losses, that is of humiliation and emptying out of all our prepossessions; (2) imagining the true worst entails the surrender of our hold on our life itself. This worst would seem to leave no one, and no hope, standing. Yet this relinquishment can also be attended by recognitions of our own evanescent mortality and of our desire to preserve the being of an other.

Such recognitions are detached from any thought of preserving our own lives. Contemplating each other in this way, the humiliated protagonists of this play struggle, in agony, to see what life-forms these recognitions of shared being can trace.

The tragic recognitions of *King Lear* depend upon exacting, interwoven propositions: namely that the process of suffering an effectively endless series of humiliations of self-conceit, even and especially including the imaginative surrender of the individual's hold on his or her life, can begin to produce the feeling of shared being; and that with the feeling of shared being comes the feeling of mutual responsibility for that shared being. In *King Lear* we are shown that all the other major protagonists who, like Lear, suffer what Cordelia calls 'the good man's distress' (4.3.18) are throughout headed not merely for a fall, but for a fission of 'huge sorrows' that will release 'ingenious feeling'. These last phrases are Gloucester's in Act 4 (4.5.268–9). We can understand the word 'ingenious' to carry both of its possible meanings simultaneously, that is, *sensitive* as well as *inventive*. Though this 'ingenious feeling' is as yet beyond Gloucester's full comprehension, it already signifies for him a sensitivity to others' pain, a capacity to 'see it feelingly' (4.5.143). And the further reach of this 'art' of both seeing and feeling – both apprehending and feeling – is that it can actually be *invented*, in the sense of being found or discovered, in the self-conscious process of experiencing 'fortune's blows'. Very much in these terms, Edgar has earlier described himself to Gloucester as:

> A most poor man, made tame to fortune's blows,
> Who by the art of known and feeling sorrows
> Am pregnant to good pity. Give me your hand;
> I'll lead you to some biding. (4.5.212–15)

'Give me your hand; / I'll lead you to some biding.' These verses recall the opening scenes of Sophocles's *Oedipus at*

Colonus – the same memorable opening that Milton was to recall at the opening of *Samson Agonistes*. Antigone says to blind Oedipus: 'rest on this rough stone . . . Come where I lead you . . . Lean your old body on my arm; / It is I, who love you'.[5] The blind, afflicted Oedipus is led toward the place and moment that will begin to spell enlightenment not only for him but for those around him. This Sophoclean precedent is itself profoundly illuminating of the capacities of the poetic-philosophical imagination to seek out the grounds of shared being. Stripped of everything worldly and with his life now at an end, Oedipus finds rest in a special biding where he is elaborately instructed that he must continue to abide during his earthly existence. This is the '*khôra*' rock of a negativity – a delimited negative space within worldly being. Sophocles's language of the *khôra* has deep affiliations with the *khôra* of negativity in Plato's *Timaeus* and, through that, with the entire tradition of apophatic thought.[6] The *khôra* signifies both *place* and *withdrawal from place*. In this double *khôra*, Oedipus, who will soon suddenly be invisibly withdrawn from this place but whose spirit will remain as protector of the place (of Athens and beyond), is to become the channel of a far-reaching blessing of being, most of all, for the community as a whole, centred in Athens. In *King Lear* intensely similar communal effects are achieved in a variety of ways that are here my principal concerns. One of these ways, we already see, is the representation of collective, un-humanised, 'unaccommodated man' – stripped of all accommodations of the human – who is led to the *khôra*-like heath. On the scene of the '*khôra*' in *Oedipus at Colonus* the hero's personal identity is dissolved into the act of blessing the being of his daughters and Athens. In *King Lear*, in a series of scenes of blessing, Gloucester and Lear each becomes the bestower of momentary blessing of being on their beloved offspring. Collaterally, Lear brings about the beginnings of a restored, communal order that intimates shared being *in extenso*.

In *King Lear* 'ingenious feeling' or 'good pity' even express themselves in a characteristic form or maxim. This is the requirement of treating all human beings as if, *a priori*, they have equal claims on nature's means of supporting being. This maxim is articulated by both Lear and Gloucester:

> LEAR: Take physic, pomp,
> Expose thyself to feel what wretches feel,
> That thou mayst shake the superflux to them. (3.4.32–5)

> GLOUCESTER: . . . distribution should undo excess,
> And each man have enough. (4.1.65–6)

It is tempting to see in these verses Shakespeare's prescient vote for socialist or Marxist ideologies. But if we take Shakespeare seriously – indeed, especially if we happen to take these ideologies seriously – we should focus on *the process of deriving* this maxim of 'good pity' for shared being through the kind of hard work initiated by this play. Otherwise, we will have only the grand sound without the grand thing. Shortly after Lear's manifesto on shaking superflux to the poor, he cries, 'Off, off, you lendings! Come, unbutton here' (3.4.97). This Lear has still not taken enough of the medicine against pomp that he prescribes. The art of sorrows in this play is supplied with an ever fuller, more persuasive, more collective, logic than Lear or Gloucester are by themselves capable of providing.

As suggested earlier, that logic begins to be provided by the effectively endless series of humiliations that the protagonists experience. This is a condition rife for the sublime and its effects. This series of humiliations is foregrounded in the successive numerical subtractions from Lear's retinue. Yet this local series of subtractions only betokens the merciless progressive reductions in the totality of Lear's and his followers' conditions of existence. Crucial for this larger form of reduction is the sense of endlessness in the repetition and continuity of the series. Thus the individual protagonist's sense of this endlessness is created in collective augmentations of consciousness that follow hard upon one another: for example, in the Fool's, Gloucester's, Kent's or Cordelia's vicarious experiences of the suffering of Lear; or conversely, Lear's slowly emerging responsiveness to the sufferings of the Fool, Edgar and Gloucester – and then of Cordelia. The so-called 'double plot' of *King Lear*, focused on the agonising running parallels between Lear's and Gloucester's fates, extends the two strands of this endlessness. In Shakespeare's representation of the series of humiliations, endlessness is thus not merely a function of the individual's extrapolations from his or her discrete experience. Rather, it is dependent on the individual's circulation of his or her experience of existence through the imagined experience of the endangered others, which is to say the others who perpetually stand endangered by death. The *epoché* or reduction in Husserl's account is in Kant's analysis of the deduction of the sublime already shown to be effected by the impact of the endless series. That impact produces a suspension of consciousness of worldly time and place, but then, crucially, discloses a consciousness of unworldly being. In Husserl's terms this is the atemporal *now* or *presence*. In *King Lear* these effects are vividly felt in the inexorable series of obliterations in the zero narrative. Yet Shakespeare also maps the climactic experience of this reduction, once again, in the almost invisible unfolding of this same reduction in the language of the 'nothing'.

Towards the Language of the 'Nothing' in King Lear

As in the plays we have already discussed, comprehension of the deepest design of *King Lear* depends upon following the language complex that surrounds the 'nothing'. While the zero narrative begins to locate the condition of the 'nothing', that condition is paradoxically endowed with vast presence and pressure by the traumatic force of the language of the 'nothing'. I proceed first to Cordelia's broaching of the 'nothing', which indeed keys the entire play to the language of the 'nothing', and second to the playing out of that language – always collectively, with empathic intentionality – by her community of sufferers. There is no one tragic hero in *King Lear*.

Shakespeare assigns an astonishing firmness, a hard certainty, to Cordelia's public utterance of the 'nothing'. In an aside she had said, 'What shall Cordelia speak? Love, and be silent' (1.1.57). But then, as if she has entered a different world, she does not remain either 'silent' or hesitant. Instead, risking all, she supplies the one word that says her all, firmly. Shakespeare has left no room for imagining hesitation in her response:

> LEAR: What can you say to draw
> A third more opulent than your sisters? Speak.
> CORDELIA: Nothing, my lord.
> LEAR: Nothing?
> CORDELIA: Nothing.
> LEAR: Nothing will come of nothing, speak again. (1.1.80–5)

As the action of the play proceeds, dozens of repetitions of the word 'nothing' and its cognates will take their reinforcing or contrastive force from Cordelia's opening pronouncement. The experience of the play as a whole will make it possible for us to grasp that, far from being disdainful of Lear's deepest human desires, Cordelia here provides him and his kingdom with the key term for the fulfilment of precisely the design that he is thwarting – the division of the kingdom that will effect a shared consciousness. Thus against the darkness that envelops Lear at the play's opening, the pronouncement of this 'nothing' is Cordelia's *imitatio* of a world-creating fiat. At this moment she is already setting out on the work that she will later be able to explain to Lear, retrospectively. Echoing Christ's words at Luke 2: 49, she will say, 'O dear father, / It is thy business that I go about' (4.4.23–4). With her opening, piercing, utterance – her unworldly 'nothing' – against the darkness of the worldly 'nothing' in which Lear is blindly immersed, she creates a counter-language in which both division of the kingdom and the labour of shared being can begin to emerge.

From the very beginning this Lear is gripped by his own anxiety of the nothing in his imminent loss of his divine right to election or chosenness. He is about to become what Solarino in *The Merchant of Venice* calls being 'worth nothing'. This – perhaps this above all – is what so enrages him in Cordelia's addressing her 'nothing' to him, touching, thereby, the publically exposed nerve of his anxiety of the nothing. Lear's love-test and attempt to hold on to the divided kingdom and to his would-be safe havens within it are attempts to negate that becoming nothing. At great cost to him and to herself, Cordelia will show him how deferring to an unworldly nothing can begin to provide continuance of the self, of being, in another mode.

For Shakespeare in *King Lear*, the experience of the unworldly nothing is much the same as it is for philosopher Kant. Kant, too, was centrally concerned with the power of the mind to experience and to make use of what he called 'cessation in nothingness (=O=*negatio*)'. Only alternation 'between reality and negation, or rather a transition from one to the other', he wrote, 'makes every reality representable' (*CPR* B 183–4). Through the experience of a specific kind of negation in the sublime the mind can gain an incomparable 'extension' and 'might' of the freedom that is a precondition for the achievement of human personality (*CJ* 5:269, 208–9).[7] For Shakespeare the experience of the unworldly 'nothing', and of transformation within that experience, are for the individual never at the level of full discursive articulation. In Shakespeare's representation of the community's speaking of the language of the 'nothing' he harnesses theatre's magic of appearance and disappearance, presence and absence. We experience this intensified, recurring theatrical sleight of hand when the actor who plays Edgar says, 'Edgar I nothing am', thereby plunging himself into a whirlpool of cessation in nothingness. Lear does the same, though differently, when he echoes Cordelia in distraction, 'No, I will be the pattern of all patience. / I will say nothing' (3.2.35–6). These utterances are in the first place generated by the waves of the zero narrative that sweep the minds of these protagonists toward momentary annihilations. Here, repeatedly, these individuals speak, and partly hear, this language together, in a community of which they themselves are only fragmentarily aware.

Juggling the 'Nothing'

In *King Lear* the language of the 'nothing' continues to work in a transformable doubleness. Following the usages in earlier plays that we have examined, Shakespeare ensures that this language will be splayed between two polar opposite meanings of the 'nothing'. He does this pointedly by assigning precisely the same words concerning the 'nothing' to the two characters who stand at the opposed outer limits of the play. Cordelia, speaking truth to Lear and Edmond speaking lies to Gloucester signify two antithetical universes of meaning when they each say, 'Nothing, my lord' (1.1.182; 1.2.31).[8] Ahead of everyone else besides Cordelia, the Fool knows the power of this antithesis.

Since the Fool is in this play the officer appointed to afflict Lear with the full depth of non-sense, it is brilliantly fitting that he should have a key role in furthering the two-edged meanings that throughout this play accompany 'nothing', 'naught' and even 'o'. In language that is full of contortions he excoriates Lear with the contrast between Cordelia's and Goneril's *saying nothing*:

> I had rather be any kind *o'thing* than a fool, and yet I would not be thee, nuncle; thou hast pared thy wit o'both sides and left *nothing* i'th' middle . . . Now thou art an O [i.e. zero] without a figure. I am better than thou art now; I am a fool, *thou art nothing*. [*To Goneril*] Yes, forsooth, I will hold my tongue, so your face bids me, though you say *nothing*. (1.4.145–55; emphases added)

The Fool's word games here boggle the mind and turn it upside down by reducing the worldly everything, which Goneril speaks, to 'nothing'. Having done this, he will soon proceed to explicate the fullness of the unworldly 'nothing' spoken by Cordelia.

Virtually from the beginning, Shakespeare locates the Fool in the position of an omniscient onlooker.[9] Although the Fool does not appear in the play till late in Act 1, he has full awareness of the revolutionary inversions that Cordelia's saying 'nothing' has brought about. In addition, he even minutely echoes (to the disguised Kent) the words that Kent spoke when Lear banished both Cordelia and Kent. Kent had there said, 'Freedom lives hence, and banishment is here' (1.1.175). The Fool echoes this reversal – which (characteristically for this play) the Fool has not heard but which hangs in the play's communal air for all to breathe – when he says of Lear, 'this fellow has banished two on's daughters and did the third a blessing' (1.4.88–9). Lear's 'banished' daughters, Goneril and Regan, are indeed 'here', while the 'blessing' of Cordelia that the Fool names begins to materialise forthwith in Cordelia decamping as Queen of France. In addition, his words prophetically see ahead to the ultimate emergence of scenes of reciprocal blessing between Lear and Cordelia, as well as between Gloucester and Edgar. Later in Act 1 the Fool adopts the perspective of 'topsy-turviness' that, as commentators have observed, rules or misrules in much of the play. His juggling of topsy-turviness provides the first decrypting of the unworldly nothing in this play. Kent, comprehending markedly less that the Fool at this point, says of the Fool's instructive 'speech' (1.4.100) to Lear, 'This is nothing' (1.4.113). But the Fool's 'nothing' is perfectly apposite to the simplicity and truthfulness of Cordelia's 'nothing' declared, she says, 'according to my bond' (1.1.88).

Cordelia's 'nothing' has spoken more than she can possibly put into words, and it (like the Fool's 'nothing' that Kent fails to comprehend) is prophetic of the actions of the *whore* sisters who will keep Lear *out-a-door*. Here, already, we have a first intimation of what a logic of *reasoning not the need* (2.4.257) might be and how its kind of calculus can produce 'more / Than two tens to a score':

> Mark it, nuncle.
> Have more than thou showest,
> Speak less than thou knowest,
> Lend less than thou owest,
> Ride more than thou goest,
> Learn more than thou trowest,
> Set less than thou throwest;
> Leave thy drink and thy whore,
> And keep in-a-door,
> And thou shalt have more
> Than two tens to a score. (1.4.102–12)

Thus absolutely commonplace – pure 'nothing' indeed – as it is in a world of sophisticate wisdom, this simple-minded speech liberates the 'nothing' of mere truthfulness from the nothingness of degenerate worldly moorings. It sends that 'nothing' floating into the atmosphere of a world that is transcendentally elsewhere.

The Fool initiates us into the lexical, visual and even typographical game with *nothing* and the *o* that runs wide and deep in this play. As if we are in the Fool's topsy-turvy head, we see O's, rounds, circles, sockets, wheels, everywhere we look; these seem to be saying something to us or to be looking askance at us, squinting. As spectators, we are put into something like the position of the apparently deranged Lear who says to Gloucester and his 'bleeding rings' (5.3.180), 'Dost thou squiny at me?' (4.5.134). We – all of us – are gradually made to feel that we, too, are beginning to see things or to read desperately into them. As if in a phantasmagoria, Gloucester's bleeding rings have already been sighted, by him, as portentous black holes in the sky, 'eclipses in the sun and moon' (1.2.91). Slowly, ceremoniously, stocks – wooden o's – are locked onto Kent's feet (2.2.114–34). Lear, as we noted, is twice pictured in the condition of being bound to deadly wheels (2.4.65–6; 4.6.43–4).

Perhaps the most penetrating components of this language of the nothing are its smallest, least noticeable units, the 'o' or 'oh'. In Shakespeare's orthography and phonology in *King Lear* the equation of 'Oh' with zero is always a gaping possibility. Like all of the other usages of the nothing in *King Lear*, these 'oh's cut two ways. 'Thy sister's *naught*. *Oh* Regan'. Lear will cry out to the other empty shell, another naught, who progressively drives him to humiliation (2.2.126; emphases added). Shakespeare's word game here with the 'Oh' that is tied on Regan is not concealed from the reader. Gloucester will later unknowingly confirm this specific instance of the game with 'Oh' by calling Regan, too, '*Naughty*', *worthless*, *wicked* (3.7.38; emphasis added). In the opposite direction, the 'O' of Cordelia's 'O look upon me, sir, / And hold your hand in benediction o'er me' (4.6.54–5) sounds, and plumbs, the unworldly 'nothing' of humility.

The 'Nothing' of Chiasmus, Once Again

Shakespeare has made it emphatically clear that in this play the access to the experience of the unworldly 'nothing' is gained through a tortuous and tortured language of the nothing:

> KENT: Nothing almost sees miracles
> But misery. (2.2.148–9)
>
> EDGAR: Edgar I nothing am. (2.3.21)
>
> EDGAR: Welcome then,
> Thou unsubstantial air that I embrace:
> The wretch that thou hast blown unto the worst
> Owes nothing to thy blasts. (4.1.7–10)
>
> EDGAR: In nothing am I changed
> But in my garments. (4.5.8–9)

These placements of the nothing seem to spell repudiations of the world. Yet in this language, even and especially in the twisted structures that give expression to its unworldly 'nothing', there is also potential a vast consciousness of the 'presence' of being. This is crucially the case because the deduction or reduction of the *epoché* of chiasmus can, with the aid of one more crucial ingredient, reveal the core of the consciousness of being – its presence – within the residuum of the 'nothing'. That ingredient, once again, is the intentionality of an awareness of the imminence of death, anxiously directed toward the other.

In the experience of chiasmus and the 'nothing' in *King Lear* Shakespeare unfolds and focuses on a multiplex dimension of collective, reciprocal intentionality. This corresponds to the intentionality that Husserl explained is indispensable for the consciousness of any object, but it works a sea change of difference from Husserl's schema in the displacement of an ego-centred consciousness. Indeed, it achieves the kind of radical intersubjectivity that Fink and Schütz projected as a necessary supplement to – actually a decisive revision of – Husserl's schema. In *King Lear* these increments of consciousness are enabled by a collective chiastic thinking.

In its rounded quadrature, chiasmus always tends to mark itself as both apothegm and apostrophe, both of which are directed towards – intended for – an absent addressee or one who abides on the borderline of life/death. In the chiasmata of *King Lear* Shakespeare leaves no doubt about the apo-strophic (*turning away*) and apo-thegmatic (*speaking out*) *projectile force* of the unworldly nothing that chiasmus produces, projected toward the community of otherness. In the linkage of cases of such chiasmus in *King Lear* each addressee is the lost or *in extremis* object of the speaker's speaking out (i.e. Gloucester for Edgar as well as for Kent; Lear and Cordelia for Kent; Kent and Lear for Cordelia). In all these cases, the intended, ultimate goal is the matching of shared consciousness of being with others in the space of the unworldly 'nothing'.[10] Here the no-place and no-time of *apo-strophe* and *apo-thegm* – turning *away* from present place and time – open toward the collective addressees and the felt presence of humanity. In Edgar's and Cordelia's symmetrical cases the goal of sharing in consciousness of being, in the space of negativity, will for a moment be realised in the chiastic expressions of reciprocal blessing. Considered from the point of view of Shakespeare's evolving mastery of the form of chiasmus, this further development – albeit still theatricalised and representational – parallels the advance from representation of the consciousness of single, inward being, as in *Hamlet*, to the representation, as in *As You Like It*, of an intersubjectivity, a shared consciousness of being in reciprocal, intentional blessing. Blessing of this chiastic kind represents the performance of reciprocal intentionality toward being. In this way Shakespeare begins to achieve his equivalent of Sophocles's disclosures of blessing in the *khôra* of negativity that are central to the achievement of *Oedipus at Colonus*.

From Lone Chiasmus toward Shared Intentionality

With a collective perspective in mind, we understand that when Edgar says, '[A] Edgar [B] I [B] nothing [A] am' (2.3.21) he is unawares amplifying Cordelia's 'nothing'. Edgar's speaking of this 'nothing' is an inversion of mere negation that is – as I have suggested of Cordelia's 'nothing' – a human version of a *creatio ex nihilo* from this 'nothing'. It also imitates the substantiality in God's self-naming, 'I am that I am', '*ego sum qui sum*' (Exod. 3: 14), and, in the meditative sphere, anticipates Descartes's cogito by two decades. When Edgar says, 'In nothing am I changed' we can begin to take the hint that *he is actively changed in the nothing*, and that that change extends to far more than his garments (4.5.8ff.). We can then glimpse, as well, that he very much 'owes nothing' – owes his gains of personality, of being – to the 'nothing' that the blasts of fortune have blown upon him and that Cordelia has already named and exemplified (4.1.1ff.)

A similar supplementation of Cordelia's 'nothing' is heard in Kent's '[A] Nothing [B] almost sees [B] miracles / But [A] misery' (2.2.148–9). The painful 'nothing' claimed by Cordelia escapes worldliness by opening a space of the negative – a miracle of un-worldliness incised within the world in privation. This visionary power of the 'nothing' is an almost physical seeing of what is invisible. This is the miracle of the 'nothing' that is disclosed as a kind of revelation within Kent's chiastic language. Thus the disinterested adherence to virtue that this 'nothing' in 'misery' makes richly possible is performed by 'poor' Cordelia's loving 'according' to her 'bond' (1.1.72, 88). We can now see that the setting for this bond is constructed by the bonding of her chiastic language (with an as yet blind Lear) at the very beginning:

> LEAR: What can you say to draw
> A third more opulent than your sisters? Speak.
> CORDELIA: [A] *Nothing*, my lord.
> LEAR: [B] *Nothing*?
> CORDELIA: <u>*Nothing*</u>.
> LEAR: [B] *Nothing* will come of [A] *nothing*, speak again.
> (1.1.80–5; emphases added)

The median 'nothing' (here underlined), which seems superfluous in the AB:BA pattern, directly names the midpoint space of the nothing within this arch chiastic disposition of 'nothing'. In the space of the unworldly nothing, revealed in the chiastic reduction, human goodness is freed to emerge. Yet Shakespeare emphasises that this intentionality of the nothing *toward being* is only enabled by the acknowledgement to oneself of the always imminent death of self as well as other. This is the death-awareness (of her self as well) that Cordelia contemplates in – and directs reciprocally towards – the Kent who has risked his life to safeguard Lear's endangered life: '[A] O thou good Kent, how shall I [B] live and work [B] To match [A] thy goodness? [A] My life will be [B] too short, And [B] every measure fail [A] me' (4.6.1–3). This moment of intensified chiasmus is powerful not least because it brings to bear the force of both the zero narrative and the language of the nothing. The *failure of every measure* expresses once again the condition of the 'nothing,' the 'O' without a figure in which the human can emerge.

Shakespeare holds on to these almost invisible equations with steel-trap tenacity. Thus he incorporates the power of the 'O' or the 'nothing' into the great meeting between Lear and Gloucester in Act 4. Frank Kermode remarks that the poetry of this scene is 'the boldest effort of imagination in Shakespeare' but that it 'has no narrative value'.[11] We can begin to resolve this apparent paradox by noting that this arrival in a moment of zero narrative is deepened by awareness of each other's mortality and by directing the unworldly nothing toward the sustaining of each other's being. Gloucester's blind glimpse of this other 'naught' projects – directly toward Lear – the tragedy's denouement and anagnorisis or recognition. At the climax of this scene with the Lear who 'smells of mortality' (4.5.129), Gloucester exclaims, upon seeing Lear's ruination and the careening of the world toward nothingness,

> [A] O [B] ruined piece of nature! [B] This great world
> Shall so wear out to [A] *naught* (4.5.130–1; emphases added)

In the dynamics of the sublime of this chiasmus a 'nothing' (or negativity) of both humiliation and perfect humility, as well as a shared consciousness of being, are disclosed at the core of consciousness, transformed from the degradations of the worldly 'O' and 'naught'. At this point, Lear's perception of the unworldly nothing is as yet far less seeing than that of blind Gloucester who unawares has already had the benefit of Edgar's instruction.

Benediction, Chiasmus and Intentionality

Shakespeare concretely represents the short-lived emergence of human benediction – benediction of the human by the human for all that is human – in the moments of life's total humiliation. While concealing his identity, Edgar repeatedly offers Gloucester unreciprocated gestures of blessing:

EDGAR TO GLOUCESTER: Bless thee, master. (4.1.40)

Bless thy sweet eyes, they bleed. (4.1.54)

Bless thee, goodman's son, from the foul fiend. (4.1.58)

The spectator knows that Gloucester unknowingly but powerfully directs a blessing of this kind to concealed Edgar. This occurs in the directedness of Gloucester's chiasmus to an apparently missing addressee whom he fears dead. And he effects this in an express medial 'Now' and 'O':

GLOUCESTER TO EDGAR: If [A] Edgar live, O bless [B] him.
Now, [B] fellow, fare [A] thee well. (4.5.40–1)

Shakespeare emphasises the anonymous or representative status of the parties to significant blessing. Personal intimacy is paradoxically irrelevant to such blessing, since it is performed by a disinterested self. What is blessed here, in each other – and in a shared awareness of the imminence of death, of self as well as other – is (even if only momentarily) shared being itself.

Gloucester's blessing of Edgar anticipates and prepares for Cordelia's supplication for Lear's blessing in the very next scene. Her plea is for the blessing of 'this child-changed father' (4.6.17). The phrase 'child-changed father' is usually taken to refer to the impact on Lear of Goneril and Regan's cruelty, but the effect on Lear of Cordelia's sharing of blessing is finally far more meaningful for his achievement of personality. This 'child-changed father' is now in reciprocal relation of blessing with the woman-child who now fathers him. The very same applies to child-changed Gloucester and his chiastic relation to his reciprocally blessing child.

The structure of Cordelia's plea for blessing is a formal realisation of the blessing of shared being. It is itself a chiasmus centred in the nothing of total humility and humiliation:

[A] O *look upon me*, [B] sir,
And [B] hold your hand [A] *in benediction o'er me*.
You must not kneel. (4.6.54–6; emphases added)

In Act 5, in answering chiastic form and its space of negativity, Lear at first fantasises a fulfilment of Cordelia's plea to him:

> When [A] *thou* dost [B] ask me blessing, [B] I'll kneel down
> And ask of [A] *thee* forgiveness ... (5.3.10–11; emphases added)

Only at the very end, however, in Lear's last words of a *looking directed directly to her* – and with the weight of death-consciousness pressing him towards his own death – does he finally fulfil, to the word, Cordelia's plea for 'benediction': 'O look upon me, sir'. In one of the most remarkable inventions of the entire play, Lear is made to achieve this blessing in concert with dead Cordelia's rehearsal of the nothing:

> Look on her! Look, her lips,
> Look there, look there. (5.3.284–5)

Although I do not find it recorded in the commentaries on *King Lear*, it must have been proposed, or at least felt, by many before that the very first word that Cordelia spoke to Lear in this play, the word that risked and cost everything – 'Nothing' – is the word that Lear is remembering, trying to resuscitate, with his last words. Somewhere in Lear's conscious or unconscious memory, he may well retrieve the words that he heard the Fool address to Goneril's 'face' that spoke 'nothing':

> Yes, forsooth, I will hold my tongue, so your face bids me,
> though you say *nothing* (1.4.154–5; emphasis added)

Not by Lear alone but by the saving remnant of this tragic community, only Cordelia's first utterance, 'Nothing', can now be made out on her face, her lips – parted, rounded, motionless – a breathless word saying Nothing, O: 'Look, her lips'. Only an experienced and fully imagined series of humiliations of self-conceit, such as this community shares, can conceive or access this O. Only this O can begin to open the mutual benediction of being. Here we see that benediction of being is in the directed looking upon the other not just to see his or her face (although Emmanuel Levinas is surely correct in highlighting that locus of seeing)[12] but to see from the space of negativity and the facing of the inevitability of death – of self as well as other. From that space of the negative we can reciprocally direct consciousness of being toward being. Lear looks upon Cordelia from and to the *nothing there*, from which Cordelia was looking on from the outset. Here we, too, are looking with the reduced saving remnant of this play, that is, from the unworldly nothing. From there we look upon the human worldly nothing in its condition of humiliation and annihilation. Thus this is not just Lear's and Cordelia's private two-way road. Rather it is a collective, multidirectional thoroughfare of benediction travelled, at least momentarily, by and for this community. At the tragedy's conclusion the surviving members of this community begin to take on the division of responsibility for shared consciousness of being. Cordelia's 'nothing' and 'O', first and last, begin to open this shared consciousness of being.

*

The interrelations between *King Lear* and *The Winter's Tale* have a particularly intense bearing on Shakespeare's realisation of his – and the spectator's – *now*. John Pitcher has detailed 'the visible flow between the two plays'. We see it in such things, he observes, as the 'reference in *King Lear* to being caught between a bear and a raging sea (3.4.9–11) [that] is made real in *The Winter's Tale*'. And we feel it 'in the harrowing final lines in *King Lear*' when a delirious Lear 'believes that Cordelia's lips have life in them. In the final scenes of *The*

Winter's Tale', Pitcher writes, 'when Leontes faces what he thinks is the inanimate statue of his dead wife' and believes 'that "the very life seems warm upon her lip" ... as sweet as "any cordial comfort", he thinks Hermione is breathing and tries to kiss her' (5.3.66, 76–7). Pitcher notes the 'half-hidden, bitter-sweet pun passing from "Cordelia" to "cordial"'.[13] To this we must add the massive parallel in the very openings of these plays when, in a fit of madness, a king banishes the person he most loves and brings about the death, or apparent death, of his daughter.

The adhesion of *King Lear* and *The Winter's Tale* to the now, nothing and blessing of chiasmus is exemplified by the figure of Perdita. Time the Chorus – the interrupter of chronological time in *The Winter's Tale* in the 'wide gap' of time (4.1.7) – locates Perdita in the transcendental *now*, picturing her 'now grown in grace / Equal with wond'ring' (4.1.24–5). Perdita is the spectator in *The Winter's Tale* who most closely succeeds to the Edgar of *King Lear*. Perdita, the lost one, even stands *ab extra* throughout. In spite of himself, Polixenes bears witness to her status of this kind: '*Nothing* she does or seems / But smacks of something greater than herself, / Too noble for this place' (4.4.157–9; emphasis added). She herself views herself in the scene around her as if she were a spectator: 'I see the play so lies / That I must bear a part' (4.4.626–7). When the curtain is drawn on Hermione as a statue, Perdita even calls herself an onlooker: 'So long could I / Stand by a looker-on' (5.3.84–5). Shakespeare goes further than giving a name to this onlooker status. He probes it for its structural identification of the place of nothing, its strange or wondrous interim. The 'nothing ... but' that Polixenes mentions, which means everything, is by Florizel given its complex inner meaning of an interval that is a death-like yet eternal still-ness, a sustained, atemporal present. 'When you do dance,' he says to Perdita, '[A] I wish you / A wave o' the sea, [B] that you might even do / *Nothing* but that: [B] move still, [A] still so' (4.4.140–3; emphasis added). On her part, the power of this country maid to disclose an atemporal interval is startlingly shown in her invocation of timeless Ovidian mythology – specifically importing a deep consciousness of a young woman's death – all in perfect chiasmus centred in the 'now':

> [A] O Proserpina,
> For [B] the flowers now, [B] that, frighted, thou letst fall
> [A] From Dis's wagon! (4.4.116–18)

Perdita's inner time fixes the inner time achieved by the play as a whole. This is already the strong time or *kairos* that Paulina will announce in her exclamation, ''Tis time' (5.3.99). This, as already noted, is also the choric Time that stands in the 'wide gap' of time between the cross-visitations of Sicilia and Bohemia. And we encounter the same time of the now in the chiasmus that Leontes and Paulina share in one continuous verse that thematises the *now*. When, he says, 'as she [A] lived [B] now' Paulina responds, 'As [B] now she might have [A] lived' (5.3.32).

Perdita stands at the centre of all achievement of blessing in *The Winter's Tale*. In Act 5, facing the statue, she says:

> [A] do not say 'tis superstition, that
> [B] I kneel and [B] implore [A] her blessing. (5.3.43–4)

For both parent participants, Paulina provides the visual iteration of the pattern of blessing by interposing Perdita – the Perdita of motionless motion and of an atemporal interval, the *Perdita* of *lost-ness* – both between herself and her mother and between Leontes and Hermione, saying:

Please you to interpose, fair madam; kneel
And pray your mother's blessing. (5.3.119–20)

Commentators have noted that Paulina has here provided the stage director with a kind of blocking cue. In fact, within the play's largest meanings, she has transformed blocking into *bracketing* and the *now* where *blessing* can take place.

We have seen that in *Hamlet* the bracketings of chiasmus do not open into blessing – to intentionality toward being of an other. Shakespeare seems to draw attention to this salient difference in his different terminologies for chiasmus in *Hamlet* and *The Winter's Tale*. In *Hamlet* the gravity of chiasmus is emphasised by having foolish Polonius call chiasmus 'a foolish figure' (2.2.98–9). In *The Winter's Tale* Shakespeare draws the spectator's attention to the potential intersubjectivity of the figure by echoing Puttenham's term for chiasmus, the 'cross-couple', when Leontes chiastically says to Perdita and Florizel,

> [A] I lost a couple that twixt heaven and earth
> [B] Might thus have stood, [B] begetting wonder, as
> [A] You, gracious couple, do. (5.1.131–3; emphasis added)

This cross-couple (of the houses of Sicilia and Bohemia) will beget the grace of wonder as well as at least the beginning of a blessing toward being. Shakespeare and the spectator as onlookers can see the chiastic correspondences that couple these couples as well as their standing and doing. For Shakespeare and the spectator or reader of Shakespeare's plays, the depth of onlooking is here once again dizzying. The standing and doing of this couple are as actors who are play-acting the roles of Florizel and Perdita who are play-acting the roles of having been allegedly 'sent' by Polixenes. Repeating this vision, Leontes formulates it as the heart of his desire for renewed life:

> [A] Might I a son and daughter [B] *now* [B] have looked on,
> [A] Such goodly things as you! (5.1.176–7; emphasis added)

The disclosed centre of these closely equivalent chiasmata is the 'wonder' of presence or the 'now'. This is the crucial product of the Husserlian reduction that Shakespeare performs in his own way, in fact well beyond Husserl's resources of language and meditation. Leontes does not know that he already stands in the temporality of the now that can renew consciousness of life. In the last lines of the play Leontes, addressing the Paulina who has stage managed all this theatre, will speak the chiastic language that exits the play and opens upon the spectator's more fully realised experience of the *now*:

> [A] Lead us from hence, where we may leisurely
> [B] Each one demand and answer to his part
> Performed in this wide gap of time [B] since first
> We were dissevered. [A] Hastily lead away. (5.3.152–5)

This 'away' is beyond the play and beyond theatre. The atemporal urgency of the now in the wide gap of time, as well as the unrepresented place of 'away', are experienced by the spectator both 'leisurely' and 'hastily'. As spectators we reach this strange interim when we follow the 'interchange' (1.1.23) of the chiasmus that leaves us in the now.

Doubling the Chiasmus of Theatricalisation

The denouement of *The Winter's Tale* – and of *The Winter's Tale* and *King Lear* together – is realised in the double chiasmata and their *epochés* that are made possible by 'the heavens' continuing and the 'heavens directing' (5.3.150) their 'loves'. This is to say that the heavens continue their loves not only from the aborted first half of *The Winter's Tale* but, I propose, from the tragic interdiction at the close of *King Lear*. The matrix of such doubling of chiasmata is set out, theatrically, within *The Winter's Tale* by

Perdita after Florizel has crowned her 'queen' of the sheep-shearing festival:

> PERDITA: Sir, my gracious lord,
> To chide at your extremes it not becomes me –
> O pardon that I name them! Your high self,
> The gracious mark o'th'land, you have obscured
> With a swain's wearing, and me, poor lowly maid,
> Most goddess-like pranked up. But that our feasts
> In every mess have folly, and the feeders
> Digest it with a custom, I should blush
> To see you so attired – sworn, I think,
> To show myself a glass. (4.4.5–14)

Where Hamlet saw that art must hold up a chiastic 'mirror' to nature – as in his Hecuba chiasmus of theatricalisation – Perdita's role in the sheep-shearing festival shows a chiastic 'glass' that (she does not yet know) doubles the chiasmus of theatricalisation. Hamlet employs the chiastic 'mirror' and its *epoché* to disclose his self or subjectivity. Beyond Perdita's immediate knowledge, her 'glass' traces a double mirroring that yields the possibility of an intersubjectivity.

The mirror of Perdita's outer chiasmus of self and other shows the 'extremes' of 'queen'-Perdita / 'swain'-Florizel // Florizel 'so attired' / Perdita 'myself'. Within these outward terms awaits another chiasmus, also of self and other, that is a mirror of the other mirror: *Perdita princess of Sicilia / Florizel prince of Bohemia // Florizel prince of Bohemia / Perdita princess of Sicilia*. Perdita, the closest thing to a fully achieved onlooker within these plays, thus points us to the matrix of a chiastically achieved intersubjectivity. We have seen that just such a possibility of achieving intersubjectivity by means of a double mirroring and a double *epoché* was envisioned by Husserl's inheritors in their effort to achieve the goal of an intersubjectivity that eluded Husserl.[14] Perdita is the arranger of a kind of double mirroring. Yet the promising matrix of intersubjectivity that she deploys is still formed by a theatricalisation of self and other that, near or far, she mirrors, she controls, and that expresses her lone ego. The escape from that control can only become possible in the full detachment of an onlooking *at* the plays from *outside* the plays. This is enabled by reflection on *The Winter's Tale* and *King Lear* together. That chiastic *object of reflection* is constituted by the over-chiasmus and *epoché* that these plays form with each other.[15]

King Lear and *The Winter's Tale* jointly perform, that is, an immense chiasmus. Whereas the trials of the earlier play are set in motion by the repeated utterance of the word 'Nothing' by a beloved daughter (1.1.182, 184), which causes a king's maddened outburst on the word nothing and the banishment (and ultimate death) of his daughter, the tribulations of the later play are set in motion by a king who himself first lingers madly on the word 'nothing' –

> Is this nothing?
> Why then the world and all that's in't is nothing,
> The covering sky is nothing, Bohemia nothing,
> My wife's nothing, nor nothing have these nothings,
> If this be nothing. (1.2.289–93)

This in turn generates the murderous court trial of his beloved wife together with his order of banishment/execution of his daughter. In near perfect chiastic inversion of the pattern in *King Lear*, in *The Winter's Tale* the king's daughter even utters the word 'nothing' in counterfactual counterpoint to Cordelia's earlier counterfactual 'nothing'. Cordelia's silent point, after all, is that she has everything to say about love for her father. 'I cannot speak / So well, nothing so well', speaks Perdita (4.4.360–1) in the very same vein. The effect of this cross-conversation is to create another bracketing of a strange interim, another moment of the now, for Shakespeare and the spectator of these plays. All this is remarkably managed by the onlooker author who thus begins to create an extra-theatrical object of reflection between these plays. Yet the most remarkable means for creating this extra-theatrical effect, between these plays, remains to be described.

Grafting, Nothing and Blessing

Only Shakespeare and the spectator (on a second viewing) can see that throughout *The Winter's Tale* the disclosure of a 'great difference' within chiastic form is redoubled in multiple, reciprocal mirrorings of chiasmus. The opening exchange between Archidamus and Camillo already sets out one such doubling in laying out the reciprocal visitations that will structure the plot of the play. Together, Archidamus and Camillo also unknowingly present the chiastic schematism of the 'great difference' between Bohemia and Sicilia/Sicilia and Bohemia:

> ARCHIDAMUS: If [A] *you* [*i.e. Sicilia*] shall chance, Camillo, to visit [B] *Bohemia* on the like occasion whereon my services are now on foot, you shall see, as I have said, *great difference betwixt* our [B] *Bohemia* and your [A] *Sicilia*. (Emphases added)

Camillo mirrors and enters into this reciprocity of visitations from where Archidamus left off. He *thinks* correctly but with no conception of how Sicilia will 'pay' that 'visitation':

> CAMILLO: I think this coming summer the [A] *King of Sicilia* means to pay [B] the *King of Bohemia* the visitation which he justly owes him. (Emphases added)

This is the beginning of the vast network of chiastic relations that will rule in this play and that will ultimately determine its relation to *King Lear*.

I propose that it is central to *The Winter's Tale* that at this opening moment, directly after the chiastic relation of Bohemia/Sicilia // Sicilia/Bohemia has been presented, Camillo extracts a chiastic pattern of a natural and even divinely sanctioned *grafting* from Sicilia's and Bohemia's apparently everyday actions of 'separation' and 'interchange' (1.1.22–3). Camillo cannot know, much less prevent, the 'great difference' that is about to erupt between Leontes and Polixenes. Yet in his opening rehearsal of the history of their friendship he proceeds to a meaning that overleaps the material causes of that 'great difference'. And he locates (blindly), as well, the operations of the far greater transformative 'vast' (25) that this play, and its relation to *King Lear*, will ultimately reveal. In *The Winter's Tale* this 'interchange' will be achieved in the natural grafting and growth of roots that will (after painful stunting) be duplicated in a natural grafting of branches that is endowed with transcendental and, indeed, scriptural meanings.

To begin to understand the meanings that Shakespeare attaches to grafting in *The Winter's Tale* we must take in the setting that the play provides to highlight its significance. Polixenes's account of an *artificial grafting* is one of the most often cited and – as far as Shakespeare is concerned – most seriously misunderstood touchstones in the history of aesthetics, that is, in the theory of the relation of 'art' to 'nature'. Polixenes's artificial, hierarchical model of grafting in fact serves as the anti-model that highlights the natural grafting which is the pivotal trope of the play as a whole. Here is Polixenes:

> You see, sweet maid, we marry
> A gentler scion to the wildest stock,
> And make conceive a bark of baser kind
> By bud of nobler race. This is an art
> Which does mend nature – changes it rather – but
> The art itself is nature. (4.4.92–7)

Shakespeare directly subverts the application that Polixenes claims for such grafting. Polixenes's account presumes to enlighten a supposedly ignorant, low-born Perdita, yet his words fly against him. This 'sweet maid' is neither of 'wildest stock' nor of 'baser kind'. The apparently 'gentler scion' of apparently 'nobler race' – Polixenes's boast for himself and his family line – is no whit gentler or nobler than Perdita and her family line. Of course, Polixenes cannot be faulted for not knowing who Perdita actually is. Yet his puffed up condescension, as well as the trap that Shakespeare has laid for his ignorance, cast doubt, for us, on the relevance of everything he says about the relation of art to nature. Most especially, the meaning of grafting in this play is profoundly different from anything that Polixenes imagines.

The artificial grafting that Polixenes describes is in *The Winter's Tale* distinctly one of two models of grafting, one artificial, hierarchical and imposed, the other natural, equal and spontaneous. In the model of artificial grafting a dominating, vividly phallic 'scion' is inserted into the incised cleft of the receiving 'stock'. Figure 5.1 shows an image of artificial grafting from the title page of Leonard Mascall's manual, *A booke of the arte and maner, howe to plant and graffe all sortes of trees* (1590), reprinted no fewer than ten times in Shakespeare's lifetime. In his right hand the well-dressed gentleman holds the cutting instrument with which he has opened the deep cleft in the stock.

Polixenes's wrong-headed invocation and application of this artificial grafting serves only to place in bold relief the play's alternative, pervasive application of the model of a natural grafting that is reciprocal and chiastic. In natural grafting, tree roots and/or branches of the same species spontaneously graft when they make physical contact with each other. As a result, the bark of the roots or branches is stripped away, thus exposing the vascular cambium and allowing the roots or branches to graft together and, thereby, produce

Figure 5.1 From the title page of Leonard Mascall, *A booke of the arte and maner, howe to plant and graffe all sortes of trees* (London, 1590). The book is in the Public Domain and is available, digitised, online in the Hathi Trust Digital Library.

a further branching. Figure 5.2 shows an image, also from Mascall's manual,[16] in which we see the chiastic conditions and chiastic effects of natural grafting, in roots as well as in branches. Seen here graphically is that which, we will see in a moment, Camillo will unknowingly prophesy about Leontes and Polixenes and their progeny: 'there rooted between them then such an affection which cannot choose but branch now'. I have drawn a rectangle upon the rooting together that has produced this tree and circles upon three of the branchings-together of the branches that emerge from cross-matchings

Figure 5.2 From page 75 of Leonard Mascall, *A booke of the arte and maner, howe to plant and graffe all sortes of trees* (London, 1590).

and that generate, as well, their own branchings, each as part of a chiasm around an invisible centre point.

By a chiastic art that is closely analogous to this natural grafting, the protagonists of *The Winter's Tale*, acting in equality and reciprocity, naturally redeem their consciousness of 'nature' through art. This pattern of natural grafting not only configures the whole of the play's plot (including, despite himself, Polixenes's own place within that plot) but already sets out the goal of an intersubjective consciousness. Built on chiastic reciprocity, this intersubjective consciousness can become humanity's greatest blessing. Here as so often elsewhere for Shakespeare, chiastic form expresses both the interchanging flux of sameness and difference in physical reality as well as the meditative reflection that can be applied to that interchange. In *The Winter's Tale* the art of chiasmus thus configures grafting as an intersection at a point, itself invisible, of 'separation' and 'great difference' in the physical world. This is also the unrepresentable inner point in which the 'nothing' as 'vast' can make us alive, as meditators, to a transformed *now* of coexistent being.

We can begin to offer a penultimate understanding of the significance of grafting in *The Winter's Tale*. Camillo pictures the chiastic workings of the natural grafting of roots and branches of the houses of Sicilia and Bohemia: 'in their childhoods . . . there [A] rooted betwixt them then [B] such an affection [B] which cannot choose but [A] branch now.' The grafted roots are Leontes and Polixenes. The branches that will be produced by the grafting of Sicilia-Bohemia (Camillo does not know) will be Florizel and Perdita. Camillo's words will turn out to be an oracular prophecy of everything that is destined to happen in *The Winter's Tale*, including Camillo's own being coupled with Paulina. As we shall soon explain, this prophecy also anticipates the enabling of the spectator's shared responses from a vantage point outside the play. Here is Camillo's account in full:

> Sicilia cannot show himself over-kind to Bohemia. They were trained together in their childhoods; and there rooted betwixt them then such an affection which cannot choose but branch *now*. Since their more mature dignities and royal necessities made separation of their society, their encounters, though not personal, have been royally attorneyed with interchange of gifts, letters, loving embassies; that they have seemed to be together, though absent; shook hands, as over a vast; and embraced as it were from the ends of opposed winds. The heavens continue their loves.
> (1.1.18–21; emphasis added)

Camillo thus sets out his understanding of a life-determining chiasmus in the way Leontes and Polixenes were thus naturally 'trained', in horticultural terms, in accordance with having a root grafting 'betwixt them': '[A] they have seemed to be together though absent, [B] shook hands [B] as over a vast, and [A] embraced as it were from the ends of opposed winds' (24–5). Yet Camillo has no grasp of the vastness of that 'vast' of 'separation,' the unrepresentable nothing, that lies waiting within this chiasmus and in which an atemporal 'now' is disclosed, that is, at the intersecting point of chiasmus figured as grafting.[17]

Paulina and Pauline Grafting

Given the heaven-directed relation of Camillo's and Paulina's own branching to the continuity of grafting in *The Winter's Tale*, we should not be surprised to discover that Paulina has an important role in placing the trope of grafting at the centre of this play. In fact, her role is even greater in this regard than Camillo's in that she points directly to the scriptural text that sets out both the special temporality of grafting and its ultimate fruit of blessing.

It has long been suggested that Shakespeare's naming of Paulina – a character who is Shakespeare's own invention – is meant to inject ideas of Paul's Epistle to the Romans into *The Winter's Tale*. A Pauline echo has been heard in Paulina's exhortation to the assembled company in the play's final scene: 'It is required / You do awake your faith. Then all stand still' (5.3.94–5).[18] We recall that in *King Lear* Cordelia invokes Christ's words at Luke 2: 49, saying to Lear, 'O dear father, / It is thy business that I go about' (4.4.23–4). I propose that in *The Winter's Tale* Paulina's exhortation to stand in awakened faith not only recalls Paul's Epistle to the Romans, 11: 20, 'because of unbelief they were broken off, and thou standest by faith', but brings with it the blessing laid out in Paul's extended simile of grafting, of which 'thou standest by faith' forms the core. Paul writes:

> *If the root be holy, so are the branches . . . If some of the branches be broken off, and thou, being a wild olive tree, wert graffed in among them, and with them partakest of the root* and fatness of the olive tree . . . *thou standest by faith* . . . And they also, if they abide not still in unbelief, shall be graffed in: for God is able to graff them in again . . . How much more shall these, which be the natural *branches*, be graffed into their own olive tree? . . . So all Israel shall be saved: as it is written, There shall come out of Sion *the Deliverer . . . For of him, and through him, and to him, are all things*: to whom be glory for ever. (*King James Version*, 11: 16–36; emphases added)

Paul's simile lays out the condition of redemption or blessing that will be created in Christ's grafting of gentile believers unto Jewish believers.[19] Paulina further echoes the structure of this sacred intent in verses that have seemed to commentators oddly vague. Soon after she has said, 'It is required / You do awake your faith. Then all stand still' and ''Tis time' she adds, as if to Hermione alone:

> Bequeath to death your numbness, for from him
> Dear life redeems you. (5.3.102–3)

Editors of the play have glossed the perplexing pronoun 'him' as *death*. Yet the word 'redeems' suggests heavier freight for 'him'. I suggest that this 'him' takes us back to the resounding transcendental coda of Paul's elaboration of the efficacy of grafting in faith. Paulina's 'from him' points, once again, to the above passage from Paul where he ends with the Deliverer's power to redeem, to save, to give 'dear life' in place of death, specifically redeeming the death of the spirit: '*For of him, and through him, and to him, are all things.*' Through

Paulina's invoking of this 'him' we have exited theatre and entered a transcendental realm of redeemed 'dear life' that is beyond worldly time and earthly representation. Yet not even the Pauline Paulina could see or represent the further Shakespearean intention in the art of chiasmus that configures grafting as an intersection at a point of 'great difference' or *epoché*. This takes place in the point of intersection between *King Lear* and *The Winter's Tale*. At the unrepresentable inner point within this grafted chiastic object of reflection – made from reflection on the two artefacts together – the 'nothing' as 'vast' makes us alive, as meditators, to coexistent being. This coexistent being extends, not least, to intersubjective coexistence with Shakespeare. This is converted, realised experience of the highest order.[20] This ultimate blessing of a grafting between the two plays emerges in the chiastic point of a *nothing* that now affords the onlooker-spectator, with onlooker-Shakespeare, a blessing in consciousness itself. The reciprocities of this blessing transpire in a *now* that has been made possible by theatricalisation but that exits theatricalisation. Here, finally, the intentionality toward being is the realised intersubjective experience of the playwright and the spectator – and all such future spectators.

Notes

1. Here it is worth recalling T. S. Eliot's remark about 'the error of presenting the work of Shakespeare as a series of mystical [or philosophical] treatises in cryptogram, to be filed away once the cipher is read; poetry is poetry, and the surface is as marvelous as the core.' Coming as it does in Eliot's introduction to G. Wilson Knight's *The Wheel of Fire: Interpretations of Shakespearean Tragedy* (New York: Meridian Books, 1957), p. xx, the remark says far more than Eliot consciously intended. I propose that the special power of the poetry of *King Lear* is in large part attributable to the fact that here the

cipher – the zero or nothing that needs to be read and marvelled at – is both surface and core. This openly inscribed, not encrypted, cipher is at the core and the surface of a meaning that is at once poetic and philosophical, aesthetic and ethical.
2. Kenneth Burke, 'Literature as Equipment for Living', in *The Philosophy of Literary Form*, 3rd edn (Berkeley: University of California Press, 1974), pp. 293–304.
3. I wish to acknowledge at the outset that to some extent this interpersonal, plural emergence and rebirth will, in its very nature, necessarily remain beyond the reach of any single, first-person perspective, including that of any literary critic. Yet if we locate the theatrical power of Shakespeare's representations of his collective narrative and collective language, this obstacle, I believe, can be partially, or momentarily, overcome.
4. My citations from the play are from *The Tragedy of King Lear*, ed. Jay L. Halio (Cambridge: Cambridge University Press, 2005).
5. The extended opening scene is elaborately centred on the *khôra* and the settling of Oedipus onto its holy rock. I quote from Robert Fizgerald's translation in Sophocles, *The Oedipus Cycle: An English Version*, trans. Dudley Fitts and Robert Fitzgerald (New York: Harcourt Brace, 1977), lines 19, 183, 200–1.
6. I have discussed the *khôra* of *Oedipus at Colonus* in 'The Emergence of Oedipus's Blessing: Evoking Wolfgang Iser', *Partial Answers* 7.1 (2009): 63–85, especially 75–6. On the negativity of the Platonic *khôra* see Jacques Derrida, 'How to Avoid Speaking: Denials', trans. Ken Frieden, in *Languages of the Unsayable: The Play of Negativity in Literature and Literary Theory*, ed. Sanford Budick and Wolfgang Iser (New York: Columbia University Press, 1989), pp. 3–70, especially pp. 31–54.
7. Cited from *Critique of Pure Reason*, trans. Norman Kemp Smith (London: Macmillan, 1993). The Third Critique is here cited from *The Critique of Judgement*, trans. James Creed Meredith (Oxford: Clarendon, 1973).

8. Edmond's signifying of the empty worldly nothing will soon find a dead echo in Macbeth's words describing the doings of his world as a 'tale / Told by an idiot, full of sound and fury, / Signifying nothing' (5.5.25–7).
9. Emily Sun, *Succeeding King Lear: Literature, Exposure, and the Possibility of Politics* (New York: Fordham University Press, 2010), p. 35, notes salient aspects of the Fool as spectator, though she does not seem to see his transcendental role, specifically as spectator.
10. Shakespeare's chiasmata of the nothing represent the causal relation of intentionality to consciousness of being and thus as a productive activity of epistemology, a creation of consciousness such as Husserl formulated. Heidegger departed from Husserl toward an ontological and non-representational understanding of intentionality as a mode of Being (*'Dasein'*) that by itself already contains the awareness effected by intentionality. The difference between Husserl and Heidegger on this fundamental point has been explored by many commentators. An accessible discussion of these matters is provided by Sean McGovern, 'The Being of Intentionality', *Lyceumblog*, new issue 9.1: 2–17. See also note 18 of Chapter 1 above.
11. Frank Kermode, 'Introduction to *King Lear*', in *The Riverside Shakespeare*, ed. G. Blakemore Evans et al. (Boston: Houghton Mifflin, 1974), p. 1252.
12. See Emmanuel Levinas, *Ethics and Infinity: Conversations with Philippe Nemo*, trans. Richard A. Cohen (Pittsburgh: Duquesne University Press, 1985).
13. *The Winter's Tale*, ed. John Pitcher (London: Bloomsbury Arden Shakespeare, 2010), pp. 19–20. My citations from the play are from *The Winter's Tale*, ed. Susan Snyder and Deborah T. Curren-Aquino (Cambridge: Cambridge University Press, 2007).
14. See Alfred Schütz, 'The Problem of Transcendental Intersubjectivity in Husserl (with Comments of Dorion Cairns and Eugen Fink)', trans. Fred Kersten, in *Schützian Research* 2 (2010): 47. In this achievement of a 'second *epoché*' in the double mirroring of intersubjectivity Fink and Schütz see an

indispensable role of the mutual directedness of an awareness of death, in both self and other, in which 'the transcendental subject must constitute itself and Others' in consciousness of 'the finitude of human being, the human fate of death' (51). This, too, is clearly in evidence, in the ever-present awareness of past or imminent death (e.g. of Cordelia, Mamillius, Antigonus) that hangs over both *King Lear* and *The Winter's Tale* and that frequently finds expression in the *epochés* of their chiasmata.

15. Eugen Fink, *Sixth Cartesian Meditation: The Idea of a Transcendental Theory of Method*, trans. Ronald Bruzina (Bloomington: Indiana University Press, 1988), p. 48, describes a second-order 'phenomenology of the phenomenological reduction' in 'making of the action of reduction the object of reflection'.
16. Leonard Mascall, *A booke of the arte and maner, howe to plant and graffe all sortes of trees* (London, 1590), p. 75.
17. Editors have glossed the 'over-kind'-ness of which Camillo speaks in many ways. I suggest that it most naturally points to the inescapable bond of nature in which they are mutually intertwined. This 'kind'-ness equally rules Leontes's and Polixenes's lives and will rule as well – Camillo cannot yet know – the lives of their offspring. In addition, as we have noted, Camillo cannot yet know that the branch grafting from the root branching that he has described will include the 'match' of himself with Paulina. Shakespeare makes these larger connections unmistakable by inscribing a host of ancillary, smaller connections. In the first scene of the play Archidamus predicts to Camillo that 'we will be justified in our loves' (1.1.8). In the last scene of the play Leontes makes the match of Camillo and Paulina, saying that it is 'here justified / By us, a pair of kings'. Similarly, in the first scene Camillo ends his account of Leontes's and Polixenes's root grafting 'that cannot choose but branch now' with the prayer, 'The heavens continue their loves.' In the last scene we hear from Leontes that the root grafting by this 'pair' here branches yet further – in the attained 'now' of chiastic grafting – by 'heavens directing' (5.3.145–6, 150).

18. An extended argument in this vein is provided by Ken Jackson, '"Grace to Boot": St. Paul, Messianic Time, and Shakespeare's *The Winter's Tale*', in *The Return of Theory in Early Modern English Studies*, ed. Paul Cefalu and Bryan Reynolds (New York: Palgrave, 2011), pp. 192–210. Jackson relies heavily on Giorgio Agamben's *The Time that Remains: A Commentary on the Letter to the Romans*, trans. Patricia Dailey (Stanford: Stanford University Press, 2005), which reads Romans through the lens of Walter Benjamin's concept of messianic time – a concept that was itself influenced by Husserl's exposition of the *epoché*. On significant points of correspondence between Shakespeare's thinking and Paul's see Julia Reinhard Lupton, *Citizen-Saints: Shakespeare and Political Theology* (Chicago: University of Chicago Press, 2005), pp. 21–48. On the relation of Benjamin's *Jetztzeit* to Husserl's thinking see note 18 of Chapter 2.

19. It has been noted by biblical commentators that Paul has here borrowed an early Jewish midrash that was later recorded in the Talmud (tractate Yibamoth 63a). That midrash glosses the phrase from Genesis 12: 3 in which Abraham is told by God 'and in thee shall all families of the earth be blessed'. The Hebrew word for *and shall be blessed* is ונברכו. The midrash turns on reading the root of this word, ברכ, as that of the Hebrew variant for grafting, הברכה, which thus yields the astounding meaning not that the grafting will lead to blessing but that the grafting is blessing itself. 'R. Eleazar . . . stated: What is meant by the text, *And in thee shall the families of the earth be blessed*? The Holy One, blessed be He, said to Abraham, "I have two goodly shoots to engraft on you: Ruth the Moabitess and Naamah the Ammonitess".' In Romans, Paul's eleven, packed verses laying out his extended simile of the grafting of gentile and Jewish believers is thus itself a grafting of Christian and Jewish texts as well as of all who stand by faith. In Judaism, spiritual identity is passed on matrilineally. From Naamah the Ammonitess, wife of Solomon, righteous queen of Israel, will come Solomon's royal successor Rehoboam. From Ruth the Moabitess will come the

prophesied Deliverer. Neither Rabbi Eleazar nor Saint Paul spelled out how grafting might in itself be blessing or deliverance. Whether or not Shakespeare knew the grafted Jewish origin of Paul's metaphor of grafting, Shakespeare finds his way, resonating with Paul, to produce blessing from the structures of grafting.

20. Here I recur to Frank Kermode's observation, in his Introduction to *The Winter's Tale* (New York: New American Library, 1998), p. lxxvii, concerning *The Winter's Tale*, that 'we value it not for some hidden truth, but for its power to realize experience'.

RETROSPECT

Philosophers lately speak of newly accessed ways of knowing reality as epistemological shifts. Clearly, Kant and Husserl proposed just such shifts in their elaborations of the terms that I have employed in elucidating Shakespeare's late practices of theatricalisation. Remarkably enough, Shakespeare exceeds the proposals of the philosophers. He anticipates and already brings to a working consummation a systematic access to the ways of knowing reality that they contemplate. In, and through, the drama of consciousness played out in the pairs of plays we have examined, the playwright and the spectator attain to an onlooker consciousness that exits the fictionality, the play-acting, of theatricalisation, and they are enabled to recover the actuality of objects in their worlds. This is no small or merely local blessing. A place to stand outside the theatricalisation of these plays is also a vantage point for achieving – as if in a new kind of catharsis – a place outside the perpetually imagined theatricalisations of everyday life. In closing these pages, a moment of retrospection on this onlooker consciousness is in order.

We have seen that Shakespeare's disclosures in his drama of consciousness begin with facing the imagination's deeply inherent theatricalisation. This is the back-and-forth movement between role-playing consciousness and a would-be non-role-playing consciousness that is never free from role-playing. The mirror that Hamlet, speaking to the player, holds up to the theatricalisation of theatre – as well as to our theatricalisation of 'Nature' – reveals that this back and forth always generates a forth and back, thus forming the omnipresent chiasmus of theatricalisation. It goes almost without saying that the 'all for nothing' at which Hamlet rates the chiasmus of theatricalisation – archetypically in the Hecuba chiasmus – is also a potentially devastating assessment of the play *Hamlet* as well as the whole of Shakespeare's theatrical output. Yet the same 'all for nothing' is by Shakespeare already being revalued far differently as the emergence, in chiasmus, of the space of negativity that will have multiple creative functions. Hamlet will himself gain awareness of some of these functions. He will achieve a perception of the 'now' that is the atemporality of the space of negativity within chiasmus, and he will feel that it is there that he himself can escape theatricalisation, can disclose a self that is apparently not theatricalised – a 'that within which passes show'. These are phenomena that are indeed explained by concepts such as the *'epoché'* and the 'now' that Husserl saw as the effect of 'bracketing' in the 'phenomenological reduction', and they are illuminated as well by Kant's idea of a 'check to the vital forces' that, in the 'deduction' of the sublime, 'removes the time condition'. These phenomena, certainly, are preconditions for achieving what Husserl calls the condition of 'onlooker' consciousness. Hamlet provides a brilliant test case for such concepts. Yet the limitations of these very concepts, in or by themselves, are suggested by Hamlet's painful inadequacies in playing them out. For Hamlet the disclosure of his inward self remains confined, almost imprisoned, within his lone subjectivity. Hamlet's endgame, however, is not Shakespeare's. From Hamlet's profound but limited discoveries of a consciousness beyond theatricalisation, Shakespeare gradually advances to a series of further increments of consciousness. These, too, are all enabled by the instrumentality of chiastic theatricalisation that Hamlet set in place. Shakespeare repeatedly moves forward to the complex and difficult idea that sharing the space of the negative within partnered chiastic relation (even if still only within theatricalisation) can begin to produce an intersubjectivity and a reciprocal intentionality toward sustained being. Here the onlooker begins to come into existence – or coexistence. To produce the full condition of the onlooker Shakespeare employs a final increment of chiastic theatricalisation that exits theatre itself. Astonishing in its intricate management of the forms of theatricalisation, this exit is produced by the chiastic juxtaposition of the chiasmata of theatricalisation in the pairings of these plays. The product of this juxtaposition that is accessed by the playwright and the spectator is an object of reflection that is outside theatre. If Shakespeare had not followed this process, in detail, at least these three times, it might seem hard to credit even for the multilayered complexity of his genius. As onlookers to these plays, Shakespeare and the spectator overleap theatricalisation to attain a goal that has all along been deferred beyond any Act five of these plays. In absolute quiet, without philosophical announcements, the playwright and the spectator have been transformed into onlookers of the object of reflection. They have relocated themselves in the invisible space, the point of 'great difference', the 'nothing' as 'vast', within the grafting of shared being. Here, in the 'nothing' of an 'un-humanising' (that is by no means a de-humanising) and of a fully attained second *epoché*, such as philosophy only begins to dream, the onlooker-playwright and the onlooker-spectator have already accessed a new horizon of liberated consciousness, of actuality per se.[1]

Note

1. Another kind of retrospect is available in Domenico Morelli's painting 'Re Lear', which serves as the cover illustration for this book. Morelli (1823–1901) represents Lear at the precise moment of act five, scene 3, line 231, when he enters carrying dead Cordelia and howls like a wolf, 'Howl, howl, howl, howl!' Morelli has depicted Lear as a veritable wolf: with wolf-like snout; with animal-like ears that metamorphose from a crown; with no visible hands or legs; and with an ungainly robe that gives him an animal-like body. And Morelli's rendering of Cordelia's open lips (in my interpretation, figuring zero/'nothing' – repeating the first word she says in the play, the word that sets the whole tragedy in motion: 'Nothing') are the lips that Lear sees and reads in the same scene at lines 284–5, then immediately dies: 'Look, her lips. Look there, look there.' Thus this depiction of Cordelia's open lips, mutely articulating the nothing or *epoché*, together with the *un-humanising* (not de-humanising) of Lear, as well as the insertion of an *onlooker* at the right side of the painting, uncannily anticipates a large part of Husserl's paradigm of incremental consciousness and captures the experienced impact, beyond Husserl, of Shakespeare's scene.

BIBLIOGRAPHY

Adelman, Janet. *Blood Relations: Christian and Jew in* The Merchant of Venice (Chicago: University of Chicago Press, 2008).
Agamben, Giorgio. *The Time that Remains: A Commentary on the Letter to the Romans*, trans. Patricia Dailey (Stanford: Stanford University Press, 2005).
Aubin, Paul. *Le problème de la 'conversion'* (Paris: Beauchesne, 1963).
Bate, Walter Jackson. *Negative Capability: The Intuitive Approach in Keats* (Cambridge, MA: Harvard University Press, 1939).
Bate, Walter Jackson. *John Keats* (Cambridge, MA: Harvard University Press, 1963).
Budick, Sanford. *The Western Theory of Tradition: Terms and Paradigms of the Cultural Sublime* (New Haven: Yale University Press, 2000).
Budick, Sanford. 'The Emergence of Oedipus's Blessing: Evoking Wolfgang Iser', *Partial Answers* 7 (2009): 63–85.
Budick, Sanford. *Kant and Milton* (Cambridge, MA: Harvard University Press, 2010).
Budick, Sanford. 'Shakespeare's Secular Benediction: The Language of Tragic Community in *King Lear*', in *Religious Diversity and Early Modern English Texts: Catholic, Judaic, Feminist, and Secular Dimensions*, ed. Arthur F. Marotti and Chanita Goodblatt (Detroit: Wayne State University Press, 2013), pp. 330–51.
Budick, Sanford. 'Bracketed Judgment, "Un-humanizing", and Conversion in *The Merchant of Venice*', in *Shakespeare and*

Judgment, ed. Kevin Curran (Edinburgh: Edinburgh University Press, 2017), pp. 195–214.

Budick, Sanford. 'Hamlet's "Now" of Inward Being', in *Shakespeare's Hamlet: Philosophical Perspectives*, ed. Tzachi Zamir (New York: Oxford University Press, 2018), pp. 130–53.

Budick, Sanford. 'Shakespeare's Now: Atemporal Presentness in *King Lear* and *The Winter's Tale*', in *Entertaining the Idea: Shakespeare, Philosophy, and Performance*, ed. Lowell Gallagher, James Kearney and Julia Reinhard Lupton (Toronto: University of Toronto Press, 2021), pp. 135–64.

Budick, Sanford, and Wolfgang Iser (eds). *Languages of the Unsayable: The Play of Negativity in Literature and Literary Theory* (New York: Columbia University Press, 1989; reprinted Stanford: Stanford University Press, 1996).

Burke, Kenneth. 'Literature as Equipment for Living', in *The Philosophy of Literary Form*, 3rd edn (Berkeley: University of California Press, 1974), pp. 293–304.

Cain, Rebecca Bensen. 'Plato on Mimesis and Mirrors', *Philosophy and Literature* 36.1 (2012): 187–95.

Cavell, Stanley. *Disowning Knowledge in Seven Plays of Shakespeare*, 2nd edn (Cambridge: Cambridge University Press, 2003).

Cavell, Stanley. 'Saying in *The Merchant of Venice*', in *Shakespeare and the Law: A Conversation among the Disciplines*, ed. Bradin Cormack, Martha C. Nussbaum and Richard Strier (Chicago: University of Chicago Press, 2013), pp. 221–30.

Curran, Kevin and James Kearney (eds). *Shakespeare and Phenomenology*, special issue, *Criticism* 54. 3 (2013).

Davenport, John and Anthony Rudd (eds). *Kierkegaard after MacIntyre: Essays on Freedom, Narrative, and Virtue* (Chicago: Open Court, 2001).

Davis, William L. 'Better a Witty Fool than a Foolish Wit: The Art of Shakespeare's Chiasmus', *Text and Performance Quarterly* 23 (2003): 311–30.

Davis, William L. 'Structural Secrets: Shakespeare's Complex Chiasmus', *Style* 39 (2005): 237–58.

de Man, Paul. *Allegories of Reading: Figural Language in Rousseau, Nietzsche, Rilke, and Proust* (New Haven: Yale University Press, 1979).

de Man, Paul. *The Rhetoric of Romanticism* (New York: Columbia University Press, 1984).

Derrida, Jacques. 'How to Avoid Speaking: Denials', trans. Ken Frieden, in *Languages of the Unsayable: The Play of Negativity in Literature and Literary Theory*, ed. Sanford Budick and Wolfgang Iser (New York: Columbia University Press, 1989), pp. 3–70.

Eldridge, Richard. '"This Most Human Predicament": Cavell on Language, Intention, and Desire in Shakespeare'. DOI: <https://doi.org/10.18192/cjcs.voi5.2414>.

Eliot, T. S. *Selected Essays 1917–1932* (New York: Harcourt, Brace, 1932).

Eliot, T. S. Introduction to G. Wilson Knight, *The Wheel of Fire: Interpretations of Shakespearean Tragedy* (New York: Meridian Books, 1957), pp. xv–xxii.

Farrell, Frank B. *Why Does Literature Matter?* (Ithaca: Cornell University Press, 2004).

Fenves, Peter. *The Messianic Reduction: Walter Benjamin and the Shape of Time* (Stanford: Stanford University Press, 2011).

Fineman, Joel. *Shakespeare's Perjured Eye: The Invention of Poetic Subjectivity in the Sonnets* (Los Angeles and Berkeley: University of California Press, 1986).

Fink, Eugen. *Sixth Cartesian Meditation: The Idea of a Transcendental Theory of Method*, trans. Ronald Bruzina (Bloomington: Indiana University Press, 1988).

Freinkel, Lisa. *Reading Shakespeare's Will: The Theology of Figure from Augustine to the Sonnets* (New York: Columbia University Press, 2002).

Gasché, Rodolphe. 'Reading Chiasms', Introduction to Andrzej Warminski, *Readings in Interpretation: Hölderlin, Hegel, Heidegger* (Minneapolis: University of Minnesota Press, 1987), pp. ix–xxvi.

Greenblatt, Stephen. 'The Death of Hamnet and the Making of Hamlet', *New York Review of Books* 21 October 2004, p. 42.

Greenblatt, Stephen. *Will in the World: How Shakespeare Became Shakespeare* (New York: Random House, 2012).

Hadot, Pierre. *Exercices spirituels et philosophie antique*, 2nd edn (Paris: Albin, 2000).

Hanna, Fred. 'Husserl on the Teachings of the Buddha', *Humanist Psychologist* 23 (1995): 365–72.

Husserl, Edmund. 'Sokrates-Buddha: An Unpublished Manuscript from the Archives', ed. Sebastian Luft, *Husserl Studies* 26 (1) (2010): 1–17.

Husserl, Edmund. 'Über die Reden Gotamo Buddhos', *Der Piperbote für Kunst und Literatur* 2.1 (1925): 18–19, now in Thomas Nenon and Hans Rainer Sepp (eds), *Husserliana: Edmund Husserl Gesammelte Werke*, XXVII (Dordrecht: Kluwer, 1989), pp. 125–6.

Husserl, Edmund. *Crisis of European Sciences and Transcendental Philosophy*, trans. David Carr (Evanston: Northwestern University Press, 1970).

Husserl, Edmund. *Ideas: General Introduction to Pure Phenomenology*, trans. W. R. Boyce Gibson (New York: Collier, 1972).

Husserl, Edmund. *Ideas Pertaining to a Pure Phenomenology and to a Phenomenological Philosophy: First Book: General Introduction to a Pure Phenomenology*, trans. F. Kersten (Dordrecht: Kluwer, 1998).

Jackson, Ken. '"Grace to Boot": St. Paul, Messianic Time, and Shakespeare's *The Winter's Tale*', in *The Return of Theory in Early Modern English Studies*, ed. Paul Cefalu and Bryan Reynolds (New York: Palgrave, 2011), pp. 192–210.

Kant, Immanuel. *The Critique of Judgement*, trans. James Creed Meredith (Oxford: Clarendon Press, 1973).

Kant, Immanuel. *Critique of Pure Reason*, trans. Norman Kemp Smith (London: Macmillan, 1993).

Kant, Immanuel. *Critique of the Power of Judgment*, trans. Paul Guyer and Eric Matthews (Cambridge: Cambridge University Press, 2000).

Kantorowicz, Ernst. *The King's Two Bodies: A Study in Mediaeval Political Theology* (Princeton: Princeton University Press, 1957).

Keats, John. *The Letters of John Keats, 1814–1821*, ed. Hyder E. Rollins, two vols (Cambridge, MA: Harvard University Press, 1958).

Kermode, Frank. 'King Lear', in *The Riverside Shakespeare*, ed. G. Blakemore Evans et al. (Boston: Houghton-Mifflin, 1974), pp. 1249–54.

Kermode, Frank. 'Introduction', *The Winter's Tale* (New York: New American Library, 1998), pp. lxiii–lxxvii.

Khatib, Sami. 'A Non-Nullified Nothingness: Walter Benjamin and the Messianic', *Stasis* 1 (2013): 82–108.

Kierkegaard, Søren. *The Concept of Anxiety: A Simple Psychologically Orienting Deliberation on the Dogmatic Issue of Hereditary Sin*, trans. Reidar Thomte and Albert B. Anderson (Princeton: Princeton University Press, 1980).

Lacan, Jacques. 'Desire and the Interpretation of Desire in Hamlet', trans. James Hulbert, *Yale French Studies* 55/56 (1977): 11–52.

Lacan, Jacques. 'The Mirror Stage as Formative of the Function of the I as Revealed in Psychoanalytic Experience', in *Ecrits: The First Complete Edition in English*, trans. Bruce Fink (New York: Norton, 2002), pp. 75–81.

Lacan, Jacques. *Ecrits: The First Complete Edition in English*, trans. Bruce Fink (New York: Norton, 2002).

Levinas, Emmanuel. *Ethics and Infinity: Conversations with Philippe Nemo*, trans. Richard A. Cohen (Pittsburgh: Duquesne University Press, 1985).

Longuenesse, Béatrice. *Kant on the Human Standpoint* (Cambridge: Cambridge University Press, 2005).

Lupton, Julia Reinhard. 'Exegesis, Mimesis, and the Future of Humanism in *The Merchant of Venice*', *Religion and Literature* 32 (2000): 123–39.

Lupton, Julia Reinhard. *Citizen-Saints: Shakespeare and Political Theology* (Chicago: University of Chicago Press, 2005).

MacIntyre, Alasdair. *After Virtue: A Study in Moral Theory*, 2nd edn (South Bend: University of Notre Dame Press, 1984).

McGovern, Sean. 'The Being of Intentionality', *Lyceumblog*, new issue 9.1 new issue (2007): 2–17.

McGushin, Edward F. *Foucault's Askesis: An Introduction to the Philosophical Life* (Evanston: Northwestern University Press, 2007).

Mascall, Leonard. *A booke of the arte and maner, howe to plant and graffe all sortes of trees* (London, 1590).
Mattéi, Jean-François. 'The Heideggerian Chiasmus', in *Heidegger: From Metaphysics to Thought*, ed. Dominique Janicaud and Jean-François Mattéi, trans. Michael Gendre (Albany: SUNY Press, 1995), pp. 39–150.
Maus, Katharine Eisaman. *Inwardness and Theater in the English Renaissance* (Chicago: University of Chicago Press, 1995).
Menke, Christoph. 'Tragedy and Skepticism: On *Hamlet*', in *Varieties of Skepticism: Essays after Kant, Wittgenstein, and Cavell*, ed. Andrea Kern and James Conant (Berlin: De Gruyter, 2014), pp. 377–83.
Merleau-Ponty, Maurice. '*The Intertwining – The Chiasm*', in *The Visible and the Invisible*, trans. Alphonso Lingis (Evanston: Northwestern University Press, 1968), pp. 130–55.
Moran, Dermot. *Edmund Husserl: Founder of Phenomenology* (Cambridge: Polity Press, 2005).
Muller, Robin M. 'The Logic of the Chiasm in Merleau-Ponty's Early Philosophy', *Ergo* 4.7 (2017), DOI: <http://dx.doi.org/10.3998/ergo.12405314.0004.007>.
Nock, Arthur Darby. *Conversion: The Old and the New in Religion from Alexander the Great to Augustine of Hippo* (Baltimore: Johns Hopkins University Press, 1998; first published Oxford University Press, 1933).
Nuttall, A. D. *A New Mimesis: Shakespeare and the Representation of Reality* (New Haven: Yale University Press, 2007; first published Methuen, 1983).
Nuttall, A. D. *Shakespeare the Thinker* (New Haven: Yale University Press, 2007).
Pattison, George. 'Kierkegaard and the Sublime', *Kierkegaard Studies Yearbook* 3 (1998): 245–75.
Purdie, Rhiannon. 'Dice-games and the Blasphemy of Prediction', in *Medieval Futures: Attitudes to the Future in the Middle Ages*, ed. John Anthony Burrow and Ian P. Wei (Woodbridge: Boydell Press, 2000), pp. 167–84.
Schlapp, Otto. *Kants Lehre vom Genie, und die Entstehung der 'Kritik der Urteilskraft'* (Göttingen: Vandenhoeck & Ruprecht, 1901).

Schmitt, Carl. *Hamlet or Hecuba: The Intrusion of the Time into the Play*, trans. David Pan and Jennifer R. Rust, Intro. Jennifer R. Rust and Julia Reinhard Lupton (Candor, NY: Telos Press, 2009; Schmitt's German title was *Hamlet oder Hekuba: Der Einbruch der Zeit in das Spiel*).

Scholten-Smith, Chris. 'Some Chiastic Structures in Shakespeare's *Hamlet*', *Idiom* 46 (2010): 39–44.

Schütz, Alfred. 'The Problem of Transcendental Intersubjectivity in Husserl (with Comments of Dorion Cairns and Eugen Fink)', trans. Fred Kersten, *Schützian Research* 2 (2010): 11–53.

Shakespeare, William. *As You Like It*, ed. Michael Hattaway (Cambridge: Cambridge University Press, 2000).

Shakespeare, William. *The Merchant of Venice*, ed. M. M. Mahood (Cambridge: Cambridge University Press, 2003).

Shakespeare, William. *Much Ado About Nothing*, ed. F. H. Mares (Cambridge: Cambridge University Press, 2003).

Shakespeare, William. *Twelfth Night*, ed. Elizabeth Story Donno (Cambridge: Cambridge University Press, 2004).

Shakespeare, William. *The Tragedy of King Lear*, ed. Jay L. Halio (Cambridge: Cambridge University Press, 2005).

Shakespeare, William. *Hamlet*, The texts of 1603 and 1623, ed. Ann Thompson and Neil Taylor (London: Bloomsbury, 2006).

Shakespeare, William. *The Winter's Tale*, ed. Susan Snyder and Deborah T. Curren-Aquino (Cambridge: Cambridge University Press, 2007).

Shakespeare, William. *The Winter's Tale*, ed. John Pitcher (London: Bloomsbury, 2010).

Shakespeare, William. *Hamlet*, ed. Ann Thompson and Neil Taylor (London: Bloomsbury, 2014).

Shakespeare, William. *Othello*, ed. Norman Sanders (Cambridge: Cambridge University Press, 2016).

Shestov, Lev. 'In Memory of a Great Philosopher: Edmund Husserl', trans. George L. Kline <www.angelfire.com/nb/shestov/sar/husserl1.html>, section 1.

Sinari, Ramakant. 'The Method of Phenomenological Reduction and Yoga', *Philosophy East and West* 15 (1965): 217–28.

Smith, David Woodruff and Ronald Mcintyre, *Husserl and Intentionality: A Study of Mind, Meaning, and Language* (Dordrecht: Reidel, 1982).
Smith, Joel. 'Merleau-Ponty and the Phenomenological Reduction', *Inquiry* 48.6 (2005): 553–7.
Soncino Babylonian Talmud Yibamoth, trans. Israel W. Slotki (Teaneck, NJ: Soncino Press, 2012).
Sophocles. *The Oedipus Cycle: An English Version*, trans. Dudley Fitts and Robert Fitzgerald (New York: Harcourt Brace, 1977).
Steiner, Uwe. 'Phänomenologie der Moderne: Benjamin und Husserl', *Benjamin-Studien* 1 (2008): 107–25.
Stern, Daniel. *The Present Moment in Psychotherapy and Everyday Life* (New York: Norton, 2004).
Sun, Emily. *Succeeding King Lear: Literature, Exposure, and the Possibility of Politics* (New York: Fordham University Press, 2010).
Vickers, Brian. 'Deconstruction's Designs on Rhetoric', in *Rhetoric as Pedagogy: Its History, Philosophy, and Practice – Essays in Honor of James J. Murphy*, ed. Winifred Bryan Horner and Michael Leff (London: Routledge, 1995).
Wilkinson, Tim. 'Mirror, Mirror', *Philosophy Now* 114 (2016), URL: <https://philosophynow.org/issues/114/Mirror_Mirror>.
Wiseman, Boris and Anthony Paul (eds). *Chiasmus and Culture* (New York: Berghahn, 2014).
Zahavi, Dan. 'Husserl's Intersubjective Transformation of Transcendental Philosophy', in *The New Husserl: A Critical Reader*, ed. Donn Welton (Bloomington: Indiana University Press, 2003).

INDEX

Page numbers in *italics* refer to figures, and those with the suffix 'n' refer to notes (e.g. 15n). Play titles have been abbreviated to: *As You Like It* – AYL; *Hamlet* – Ham.; *King Lear* – Lr.; *The Merchant of Venice* – MV; *Othello* – Oth.; *Twelfth Night* – TN; *The Winter's Tale* – WT.

Abraham, 48, 152n
Adam (*AYL*), 85
Agamben, Giorgio, 152n
Antigone, 117
anti-Semitism, 37, 41, 47–8, 50, 94–5, 106, 109
   conversion (Jew to Christian), 33, 39, 41, 42–4, 46–7
Antonio (*MV*)
   anti-Semitism, 41, 42, 43, 46, 48, 94
   'hazard', 40, 42, 43
   homoerotic desire, 51n
   'worth nothing', 34–5, 36
Antony and Cleopatra, 79
anxiety of the nothing, 36, 37–8, 44, 48, 71, 121
anxious sublime, 36, 44–5
apostrophe, 9, 26n, 127
Archidamus (*WT*), 140
As You Like It, 4–5, 70–88, 127
   paired with *Ham.*, 14, 22, 63, 70–5, 78–80, 86–8, 108, 127
atemporality *see* 'now' (atemporality)
Augean stables, 62
Ausbruch (breaking out), 49–50, 63, 100, 106

banishment, 76, 86, 123, 134, 139
Bassanio (*MV*), 34, 35, 39, 40, 42, 43–4
Bate, Walter Jackson, 1
being (object of intentionality)
   blessing, 48, 111
   inward being (*Ham.*), 6–7, 55–7, 59, 61–2, 64–9, 156
   'nothing', 13–14, 15, 35–6, 38, 40, 126, 129
   'other', 50
   playwright and spectator, 18–19, 41, 105, 107, 108

being of an other (object of intentionality), 18, 24, 38, 157–8
   AYL, 81–4
   Ham., 136
   Lr., 111–12, 114–19, 121, 127–8, 130–3
   Lr. and WT, 148
   Oth., 12–13, 101–2, 104
   WT, 145
Belmont, 38
Benjamin, Walter, 50, 152n
blessing
   Lr., 112, 117, 123, 127–8, 130–3
   Lr. and WT, 146, 148
   MV, 38, 48
   WT, 135–6, 144, 146–8
blindness *see* sight and blindness
Bohemia, 135, 136, 138, 139, 140–1, 145
Booke of the arte and maner, howe to plant and graffe all sortes of trees, A, 142–3
bracketing
   definition, 9–10, 11, 15, 16–18, 33, 156
   Ham., 61, 63, 67, 69, 136
   Lr. and WT, 139
   MV, 34, 44, 45, 47–8, 106–7
   WT, 136
Bruzina, Ronald, 30–1n
Burke, Kenneth, 113

Camillo (WT), 140–1, 143, 145–6
Cassio (Oth.), 12, 96–7
catharsis, 23, 24, 155
Cavell, Stanley, 2, 22–4, 39
Celia (AYL), 73, 74, 76–7
Charles (AYL), 76, 78
Chaucer, Geoffrey, 53n
chiasmus, 9–12, 15, 20–1, 156–7
   AYL, 75–6, 77, 80–2, 83–5
   Ham., 5–9, 49, 56–64, 67, 69, 136, 138, 156–7
   Ham. and AYL, 63, 71, 79–81, 86–7, 127
   Lr., 13, 112, 126–32
   Lr. and WT, 134, 137, 139, 148
   MV, 35, 38, 45
   MV and Oth., 50, 93–4, 100, 102, 106, 107–8
   Oth., 12–13, 94, 95–7, 106
   WT, 142–3
Christ Jesus, 121, 146–7
Christians
   anti-Semitism, 37, 41, 94–5
   conversion of Jews, 33, 39, 41, 42–4, 46–8
   grafting, 147, 152n
Claudius (Ham.), 59, 62, 86
Coleridge, Samuel Taylor, 21
Commedia dell'arte, 40
conversion
   of consciousness/of the nothing, 18–19, 33–4, 36–7, 45, 50, 75
   religious (Jew to Christian), 33, 39, 41, 42–4, 46–7
Cordelia (Lr.)
   blessing, 111, 112, 117, 123, 127, 131–2, 146
   humiliation/suffering, 119
   'nothing', 4, 13, 36, 109, 112, 120–5, 128–9, 132–3, 139
   parallels in WT, 133–4, 139, 146
   spectator, 14

Davis, William L., 25n
de Man, Paul, 11, 29n, 90n
death-awareness
  AYL, 74, 76, 77–84, 87
  de Man, 90n
  Ham., 80, 87
  Lr., 119, 126, 129–33
  Oth., 12–13, 100–1
  WT, 135
deduction, 10–11, 44, 119,
  126, 156
Dekker, Thomas, 97
Denmark, 56, 58, 60, 62
Derrida, Jacques, 29n
Descartes, René, 16, 128
Desdemona (Oth.), 12, 94, 96–9,
  100–1, 102, 103–5
dice, 42, 53n
divine election, 38, 48, 121
double meanings, 61, 72, 79, 122
double mirroring, 21, 77, 138, 140
double plot (Lr.), 114–19, 127, 128
Duke of Venice (MV), 46
Duke Senior (AYL), 85

Edgar (Lr.)
  beggar disguise, 13, 114
  blessing, 13, 112, 123, 130–1
  humiliation, 115, 116, 119
  'nothing', 4, 122, 126, 128
  shared consciousness of
    being, 127
  spectator, 14, 134
Edmond (Lr.), 4, 122
ego
  ego-centredness, 3, 35, 80, 102,
    107–8
  humiliation, 113
  intersubjectivity, 19–20, 70,
    127, 139

  negation of, 1, 2
  see also self (inward being); self
    and other
Einbruch (breaking-in), 47–50,
  62–3, 100, 106
Eldridge, Richard, 26–7n
Eleazar, Rabbi, 152n
Eliot, T. S., 58, 148–9n
Elmakies, Micha, 90n
England/Englishness, 100, 105–6
entanglement, 12, 94, 96, 98
Entmenschung (un-humanising),
  18, 19, 39, 106–7, 108, 117
epistemological shifts, 155
epistrophe, 33, 42–3, 54n
epoché
  AYL, 74, 77
  definition, 9–10, 11, 15, 16–18,
    33, 156
  Ham., 61
  Ham. and AYL, 71, 87
  Lr., 112, 119, 126
  Lr. and WT, 137, 148
  MV, 44, 45, 106–7
  MV and Oth., 105
  Oth., 96, 100, 102
  see also second epoché
equipment for living, 113–14

faith, 76, 82, 146–7, 152n
falling/falls, 74, 76–8, 81,
  84–6, 116
Farrell, Frank B., 27n
Fineman, Joel, 25n
Fink, Eugen, 17–21, 77, 91n,
  127, 150–1n
Florizel (WT), 5, 134–5, 136,
  138, 145
Fool (Lr.), 114, 115, 119,
  122–5, 132

Foucault, Michel, 42–3, 54n
Frederick (*AYL*), 86
Freinkel, Lisa, 6, 11

Ganymede (*AYL*), 72, 76
Gasché, Rodolphe, 29n
Genesis, 48, 152n
Gertrude (*Ham.*), 59, 64–5
Ghost (*Ham.*), 66
Gibson, W. R. Boyce, 30n
Globe theatre, 62
Gloucester (*Lr.*)
 blessing, 13, 112, 117, 123, 130–1
 humiliation/suffering, 115, 116, 119, 125, 130
 'nothing', 129–30
 parallels with Lear, 117–18, 119, 122, 123, 127, 129–31
God, 38–9, 46, 48, 67, 105, 128
Goneril (*Lr.*), 123, 131, 132
Goodwins, 46
grafting, 141–8, 157
Gratiano, 35, 38–9, 46–7, 95, 105, 107
'great difference', 140–1, 145, 148, 157
Greenblatt, Stephen, 5

Hamlet, 5–9, 55–69
 chiasmus, 5–9, 49, 56–64, 67, 69, 136, 138, 156–7
 failed intersubjectivity, 19
 inward self, 6–7, 55–7, 59, 61–2, 64–9, 156
 irony, 23
 mirror to nature, 6, 26n, 57, 69, 138, 156
 paired with *AYL*, 14, 22, 63, 70–5, 78–80, 86–8, 108, 127

theatricalisation, 2–3, 4, 6, 7–9, 48–9, 55–7, 58–62, 67
handkerchiefs, 94, 98–9
Hanna, Fred, 29n
'hazard', game of, 37, 40–2, 47, 53n
Hecuba (*Ham.*), 2, 8, 49, 59, 61, 63, 138, 156
Hegel, Georg Wilhelm Friedrich, 6, 89n
Heidegger, Martin, 16, 150n
hell, 103; *see also* perdition
Hemmung (check), 10–11, 21, 44
Hercules (*Ham.*), 62, 86
Hermione (*WT*), 134, 135, 139, 147
Hochstein, Stephen, 26n, 28n
Honest Whore, The, 97
Horatio (*Ham.*), 8, 66, 67, 75, 78, 85
human condition, 2, 3, 109; *see also* being (object of intentionality); being of an other (object of intentionality); non-being (object of intentionality); un-humanising (*Entmenschung*)
humiliation, 4, 113, 114–16, 118–19, 125, 130, 131, 133
humility, 125, 130, 131
Husserl, Edmund
 bracketing and *epoché*, 9–10, 15, 16–18, 33, 119, 156
 intersubjectivity, 10, 14–15, 18–19, 70, 138, 156
 reduction, 18, 21, 44–5, 156
 second *epoché*, 19–21, 50, 55, 157

un-humanising (*Entmenschung*), 18, 19, 39, 106–7
Hymen (*AYL*), 4–5, 84–5

Iago (*Oth.*), 12–13, 95, 96–9, 101, 102–3, 105–6
identity, 7, 73, 76, 117, 130, 152n
intentionality, 12–13, 18, 80; *see also* being (object of intentionality); being of an other (object of intentionality); non-being (object of intentionality); reduction
intersubjectivity
  AYL, 74–6, 82, 84
  Fink and Schütz, 17–21, 77–8, 127
  Ham., 65
  Husserl, 10, 14–15, 18–19, 70, 138, 156
  Lr., 127–8
  MV, 36
  Oth., 100
  paired plays, 70–1, 79–81, 85–8, 106–7, 148
  playwright and spectator, 2, 3, 50, 56, 107–9, 112, 139–40, 155–7
  WT, 136, 138, 144
inward being *see* self (inward being)

Jackson, Ken, 152n
Jacques (*AYL*), 73
Jessica (*MV*), 40, 43, 95
Jews/Jewishness
  anti-Semitism, 37, 41, 47–8, 50, 94–5, 106, 109
  grafting, 147, 152n

as 'nothing', 39, 41, 45
pressure to convert, 33, 39, 41, 42–4, 46–7
Julius Caesar, 25n, 53n

Kant, Immanuel
  cessation in nothingness, 121–2
  Hemmung, 10–11, 16, 21, 44
  sublime, 10, 11–12, 36, 44–5, 118–19, 156
Keats, John, 1–2, 17
Kent (*Lr.*)
  disguise, 114, 123
  humiliation, 114, 115, 119, 125
  'nothing', 4, 14–15, 36, 109, 124, 126, 128–9
  shared consciousness of being, 127
Kermode, Frank, 22, 129–30, 153n
khôra, 16, 117, 128, 149n
Kierkegaard, Søren, 30n, 36
King Lear, 111–34
  double plot, 114–19, 127, 128
  'nothing', 4, 13, 14–15, 36, 109, 112, 119–30, 132–3, 139
  paired with *WT*, 5, 14, 111, 133–4, 137, 139–41, 146, 148
  presentness, 22–3
  sight and blindness, 14–15, 36, 115–17, 121, 128–30, 133

Lacan, Jacques, 25n, 88–9n
Laertes (*Ham.*), 78, 88n
Lear (*Lr.*)
  blessing, 112, 117, 123, 131–3
  humiliation/suffering, 115, 118–19, 125, 133
  'nothing', 4, 120–1, 124, 129–30
  spectator, 14–15

Leontes (*WT*), 5, 134, 135, 136–7, 139, 141, 143, 145–6
Levinas, Emmanuel, 133
lions, 76, 78, 81, 86
London, 62
Lorenzo (*MV*), 95
love, filial/parental
   Lr., 4, 112, 121, 134
   Lr. and *WT*, 137, 139
love, romantic
   AYL, 4–5, 76, 81, 82–4
   Ham., 4–5, 58
   Ham. and *AYL*, 72–5, 78, 86–7
   Oth., 100–1, 102, 103–4
Lupton, Julia Reinhard, 49

Macbeth, 150n
MacIntyre, Alasdair, 52n
Mcintyre, Ronald, 26n
madness, 7, 99–100, 125, 134, 139
Mahood, M. M., 46–7
Malvolio (*TN*), 42, 89–90n
Mares, F. H., 35
Mascall, Leonard, 142, 142–3, 143
materialism, 34–5, 38, 39, 141
Maus, Katharine Eisaman, 88n
meditation
   Ham., 6, 55, 57, 61, 69
   Lr., 128, 148
   WT, 145, 148
Menke, Christoph, 23–4
Merchant of Venice, The, 33–51, 121
   paired with *Oth.*, 45–6, 50–1, 93–6, 100, 102, 105–8
Merleau-Ponty, Maurice, 25n, 29n, 90n
Middleton, Thomas, 97

midrash, 152–3n
Milton, John, 10, 117
mirroring
   chiasmus (*Ham.*), 60, 62
   double mirroring, 21, 77, 138, 140
   double plot (*Lr.*), 114–19, 127, 128
   intersubjectivity, 3, 20–1, 77–8, 87, 108
   of nature (*Ham.*), 6, 26n, 57, 69, 138, 156
   racism/anti-Semitism (*MV*), 37, 94–5
   wrestling and death (*AYL*), 77–82
mirror-stage, 88–9n
Moran, Dermot, 32n
Morelli, Domenico, 157n
Much Ado About Nothing, 35
muteness *see* silence (muteness)

Naamah the Ammonitess, 152n
nature
   mirror to (*Ham.*), 6, 57, 69, 138, 156
   natural vs. artificial grafting (*WT*), 141–6, 147
Nazism, 48, 106
negative capability, 1–3, 14–15, 17, 58–9, 88
negativity (negative space), 6–12, 16–17, 19–20, 44, 156–7
   AYL, 75, 79, 84–5
   Ham., 6, 8, 49, 55, 57–9
   Ham. and *AYL*, 71, 88, 108
   Lr., 13, 127–8, 132, 133
   MV, 47, 49
   MV and *Oth.*, 50
   Oth., 12, 97

Nerissa (*MV*), 35, 96, 107
Nietzsche, Friedrich Wilhelm, 23
non-being (object of
  intentionality), 12–13, 15,
  36, 40, 45, 100–3, 105; *see
  also* death-awareness
'nothing', language of
  AYL, 70–1, 75, 77, 78–81, 83
  Ham., 2, 61, 156
  Lr., 4, 13, 14–15, 36, 109, 112,
    119–30, 132–3, 139
  Lr. and *WT*, 5, 139, 148
  MV, 33, 34–40, 42, 45, 95
  MV and *Oth.*, 50, 105–6
  Oth., 12–13, 94, 95–101,
    102, 103
  second *epoché*, 50, 55, 157
  WT, 134–5, 145, 148
  see also zero narrative
'now' (atemporality)
  AYL, 80
  Ham., 57, 62, 64–9, 80, 156
  Ham. and *WT*, 136–7
  of inward being, 7, 16, 18, 24,
    57, 62, 64–9
  Lr., 119, 127
  Lr. and *WT*, 133–4, 139
  outside theatricalisation, 11–15,
    24, 62, 88, 108, 148, 156
  WT, 145–6
Nuttall, A. D., 14, 52n

'o', 122, 125, 129, 130, 131,
  132–3
Oedipus at Colonus, 16, 113,
  116–17, 128
Oliver (*AYL*), 78, 81
onlookers, transcendental
  AYL, 74, 87–8
  Ham., 63–4, 69
  Ham. and *AYL*, 70
  Lr. and *WT*, 138–40, 148
  MV, 34, 37, 47, 49
  MV and *Oth.*, 45, 50, 95, 108
  steps to becoming, 18
  WT, 136
  see also intersubjectivity
Ophelia (*Ham.*), 58, 61, 71, 72,
  74, 78, 87
Orlando (*AYL*)
  'nothing', 4–5, 70–1, 78–9, 83
  play-acting, 72–4, 78–9, 82,
    83–5, 87
  wrestling, 75–7, 78, 80–1, 83,
    85, 86
Othello, 12–13, 93–108
  paired with *MV*, 45–6, 50–1,
    93–6, 100, 102, 105–8
Othello (*Oth.*), 12–13, 93–5,
  96–101, 102, 103–5
other *see* self and other

paired plays, 21–2, 37, 50–1,
  108–9, 155, 157
  Ham. and *AYL*, 14, 22, 63,
    70–5, 78–80, 86–8, 108, 127
  Lr. and *WT*, 5, 14, 111, 133–4,
    137, 139–41, 146, 148
  MV and *Oth.*, 45–6, 50–1,
    93–6, 100, 102, 105–8
Pantalone, 40
'Pardoner's Tale, The', 53n
Patanjali Yoga Sutras, 16
Pattison, George, 36, 44
Paul, Saint, 48, 146–7
Paulina (*WT*), 135–6, 137,
  146–8
Perdita (*WT*), 5, 14, 134–5, 136,
  138–9, 142, 145
perdition, 94, 98, 100

personality, 2, 4, 100, 121, 128, 131
Pitcher, John, 133–4
Plato, 16, 43, 117
play-acting
   AYL, 76, 78–9, 82, 83–5
   Ham., 6, 8, 23, 49, 56–7, 60–1, 63, 65, 67, 69, 155–6
   Ham. and AYL, 72–5, 78, 79, 87
   Oth., 102–5
   WT, 136
Polixenes (WT), 5, 134, 136, 141–6
Polonius (Ham.), 7, 59, 60, 61, 71, 136
Portia (MV), 33–4, 39, 40, 42, 43–4, 45
psychoanalysis, 25n, 74, 81–2, 89n; *see also* ego
pudendal joke, 35, 96, 107
Puttenham, George, 136

racism, 95, 100, 106, 108–9; *see also* anti-Semitism
redemption, 147–8
reduction, 18, 21, 44–5, 156
   Ham. and AYL, 87
   Lr., 118–19, 126, 129
   MV, 50
   WT, 137
Regan (Lr.), 123, 125, 131
Richard III, 53n
role-playing *see* play-acting
Romans, Epistle to the, 146–7
Rosalind (AYL)
   displaced niece, 86
   'nothing', 4–5, 70–1, 78–9
   play-acting, 72–4, 79, 82, 83–5, 87
   spectator, 14
   wrestling, 75–7, 80–1

Rosincrance (Ham.), 62
Rust, Jennifer, 49
Ruth the Moabitess, 152n

Salarino (MV), 34–5, 36, 43, 121
Samson Agonistes, 117
Sartre, Jean-Paul, 15, 16
Schmitt, Carl, 48–50, 62–3
Schütz, Alfred, 19–20, 77, 78, 91n, 127, 150–1n
scripture, Judaeo-Christian, 48, 141, 146–7, 152n
second *epoché*, 19–21, 49–50, 55, 56, 157
   Ham. and AYL, 70, 88
   MV and Oth., 93, 107–8
self (inward being)
   Ham., 6–7, 55–7, 59, 61–2, 64–9, 156
   Lr., 121, 127
   'now' of the self, 7, 16, 18, 24, 57, 62, 64–9
   see also ego
self and other
   chiasmus, 8, 35, 38, 45, 94
   mirroring, 20, 77, 138–9
   wrestling AYL, 75, 77
   see also being of an other (object of intentionality); ego
sexuality
   AYL, 74
   MV, 35, 38, 42, 96, 107
   Oth., 12, 96–7, 98, 100
Shakespeare, William
   authorial intentions, 61–2, 85, 95, 102, 107, 148
   intersubjectivity with the spectator, 2, 3, 50, 56, 107–9, 112, 139–40, 155–7
   risk/hazard, 39, 40–1

Shakespearean consciousness, 1, 5, 9–10
shared being *see* being of an other (object of intentionality)
Sharon, Carmel, 90n
Shylock (*MV*)
　complexity/humanity, 40
　conversion, 33, 39, 41, 42–4, 45, 46–7
　hatred of Christians, 37, 48
　quoted by Solanio, 95
Sicilia, 135, 136, 138, 140, 141, 145
sight and blindness
　Lr., 14–15, 36, 115–17, 121, 128–30, 133
　WT, 5, 141
silence (muteness)
　AYL, 83–4
　Ham., 63–4
　Lr., 120, 132, 139
　MV, 41, 95
　Oth., 95
Sinari, Ramakant, 29–30n
Smith, David Woodruff, 26n
Smith, Joel, 29n
social class, 114, 118
Solanio (*MV*), 95
Solomon, 152n
Sophocles, 16, 113, 116–17, 128
spectators
　characters as, 14, 134, 137–8
　presentness, 22–4
　racist 'self', 106
　superior position, 13, 131
　see also intersubjectivity; onlookers, transcendental
Stern, Daniel, 81–2
sublime
　AYL, 84

Kantian sublime, 10, 11–12, 36, 44–5, 118–19, 156
　Lr., 118–19, 121, 130
Sun, Emily, 150n
suspensions
　Ham., 7, 9, 58, 65
　Ham. and *AYL*, 86–7
　Hemmung, 10–11, 16, 21, 44
　MV and *Oth.*, 107, 108
　Oth., 100, 102
　of suspensions of disbelief, 46–7
　see also 'now' (atemporality)

Talmud, Yibamoth, 152n
temporal rupture *see Einbruch* (breaking-in)
theatre companies, 62
theatricalisation
　AYL, 81, 82, 83
　Ham., 2–3, 4, 6, 7–9, 48–9, 55–7, 58–62, 67
　Ham. and *AYL*, 71, 86–8
　Lr., 112, 127
　Lr. and *WT*, 137–40, 148
　MV, 46–7
　MV and *Oth.*, 105–8
　Oth., 102–4
　see also intersubjectivity
third, the, 33, 37, 41–4
Timaeus, 16, 117
time *see Einbruch* (breaking-in); 'now' (atemporality)
Time the Chorus (*WT*), 134, 135
topical/contemporary anxieties, 62–3, 106
transcendental onlookers *see* onlookers, transcendental
trial by jury, 46–7, 105, 139
Twelfth Night, 42, 89–90n

'ungartered' lover, 71–2, 86–7
un-humanising (*Entmenschung*),
    18, 19, 39, 106–7, 108, 117

vaginal space *see* pudendal joke
vastness, 141, 145–6, 148, 157
Venice, 35, 40, 94, 105, 108
Venice, Duke of (*MV*), 46

Winter's Tale, The, 22, 99, 133–48
    grafting and consciousness,
        141–8
    paired with *Lr.*, 5, 14, 111,
        133–4, 137, 139–41, 146,
        148
    wrestling, 74, 75–8, 80–1, 83,
        85, 86

yoga, 16

Zahavi, Dan, 31n
zero, 15, 38, 123, 125
zero narrative, 113–19, 122,
    129–30

EU representative:
Easy Access System Europe
Mustamäe tee 50, 10621 Tallinn, Estonia
Gpsr.requests@easproject.com

www.ingramcontent.com/pod-product-compliance
Lightning Source LLC
Chambersburg PA
CBHW070358240426
43671CB00013BA/2548